FAN PHENOMENA

MARILYN MONROE

EDITED BY
MARCELLINE BLOCK

Credits

First Published in the UK in 2015 by Intellect Books,
The Mill, Parnall Road, Fishponds, Bristol, BS16 3JG, UK

First Published in the USA in 2015 by Intellect Books,
The University of Chicago Press, 1427 E. 60th Street,
Chicago, IL 60637, USA

Editor: Marcelline Block

Series Editor and Design: Gabriel Solomons

Typesetting: Gabriel Solomons

Copy Editor: Emma Rhys

A Catalogue record for this book is available from
the British Library

Fan Phenomena Series
ISSN: 2051-4468
eISSN: 2051-4476

Fan Phenomena: Marilyn Monroe
ISBN: 978-1-78320-201-0
eISBN: 978-1-78320-263-8 / 978-1-78320-264-5

Printed and bound by
Bell & Bain Limited, Glasgow

🅐 intellect

Contents

Acknowledgements

I wish to express my immense gratitude to the series editor of *Fan Phenomena*, Gabriel Solomons, to whom I am most indebted, for his enlightening and visionary leadership for the entire book series, and for his involvement in every aspect of bringing this volume to fruition; without him, the book would not have happened. Working with Gabriel on this book has truly been a great privilege and honour.

All my thanks to everyone at Intellect and the University of Chicago Press for the production and publication of this volume, especially to James Campbell for selecting it for the University of Chicago Press Seasonal Sales conference, to Jessica Pennock for tirelessly organizing the book's promotional events, and to Emma Rhys for her patient, thorough and careful review of the text.

I gratefully acknowledge devoted and knowledgeable Marilyn Monroe fans Gianandrea Colombo, Jackie Craig, Scott Fortner, Marijane Gray, Tara Hanks, Melinda Mason, Megan Owen, Jim Parson, Leah Peterson, Kara Pugh, Mary Sims, as well as MM impersonators Deborah Bakkar ('Debra Monroe'), Susan Griffiths and Suzie Kennedy for lending their insight into the fascinating worlds of Marilyn Monroe fans and impersonators. Their reverence for and devotion to Marilyn is most impressive, as is their generosity of spirit in sharing items from their personal MM archives and collections that are reproduced in these pages. The inclusion of these fans' and impersonators' words, images and perspectives on MM enhances this volume. I am thankful to Tara Hanks for allowing us to reproduce an excerpt from her book, *The MMM Girl: Marilyn Monroe, by Herself...* (UKA Press, 2007), of which she holds the rights/permissions.

I am most grateful to the contributors to this volume, Raquel Crisóstomo, Louise Elali, Scott Fortner, Zachary Ingle, Ross Sloan, Catalina Vázquez and Ange Webb, whose remarkable essays are presented herewith. Thanks to all for their outstanding work.

It is an honour to be part of the *Fan Phenomena* editorial team, and I most appreciated productive dialogues with Nicola Balkind, Paul Booth and Zachary Ingle, fellow editors of other volumes in this series.

This book is dedicated to the memory of Masoud Yazdani, Founder, Publisher and Chairman of Intellect.

Marcelline Block, editor

Introduction
Marcelline Block

→ More than five decades after her passing on 5 August 1962, Marilyn Monroe - born Norma Jeane Mortenson[1] on 1 June 1926 - remains at the forefront of the American imagination, aesthetic preoccupation and modern-day mythology: an icon 'at the very center of American political and cultural life' (Carl Rollyson, *Marilyn Monroe: A Life of the Actress*). For John De Vito and Frank Tropea, Marilyn's 'legend has surpassed that of every other major Hollywood goddess [...] making her the greatest myth figure of them all' (*The Immortal Marilyn*). She is 'the WOMAN of the twentieth century' (Frederic Cabanas, *Marilyn Monroe: Una bibliografia*) - and also the twenty-first, in her fans' opinions.

Fig. 1: Settimanale Vita (Italy), August 1962, 'The Last Hours of MM' (© Private Collection Gianandrea Colombo).

Marilyn is forever imprinted in American and international folklore, and 2012, the 50th anniversary of her death, was 'to be Marilyn's year', according to Scott Fortner, a foremost figure of MM fandom. Fortner contributes a chapter to this volume entitled 'The 50th Anniversary of Marilyn Monroe's Death', in which he discusses the largest fan memorial tribute held for Marilyn, which he helped organize. 2012 was truly 'Marilyn's year', as demonstrated by the multimedia tributes to her on the big and small screens, which are examined in *Fan Phenomena: Marilyn Monroe* by Zachary Ingle in 'Performing Marilyn: Michelle Williams in *My Week with Marilyn*' and Raquel Crisóstomo's 'Marilyn is a *Smash*: Depicting the Icon in NBC's Musical Drama'.[2]

Marilyn Monroe's year witnessed innumerable commemorations: museum and gallery exhibits; magazine/newspaper articles; the HBO documentary *Love, Marilyn* directed by Liz Garbus; biographies including Lois Banner's *Marilyn: The Passion and the Paradox*; art books released by Taschen (*Norman Mailer/Bert Stern : Marilyn Monroe*; Lawrence Schiller's *Marilyn & Me: A Photographer's Memories*) and Skira (Stefania Ricci and Sergio Risaliti's *Marilyn*), among others. As Marilyn was selected to promote the 65th Festival de Cannes in 2012, her image graced the festival's posters, for a public of movie buffs, film aficionados, critics, producers and laypeople - in other words, a whole community of film industry magnates, producers, consumers and voyeurs. In 2014, Marilyn was back at Cannes: the runway of the annual Cannes amFar charity gala, Cinema Against AIDS, was painted red in her memory, recalling her signature lipstick color.

Marilyn was named 'Most Glamorous Star of All Time' by the UK Sunday *Express* (13 June 2014) and in early January 2015 it was announced that her image is to appear in Max Factor cosmetics' ad campaigns as the brand's 'global glamour ambassador'. She seems to perfectly illustrate John David Ebert's concept of the '"electronic media superstar" [...] that species of celebrity that does not become less famous with [...] time, but rather more so' (*Dead Celebrities, Living Icons*). Marilyn's 'life is over, but her story has not finished; in fact, it has flourished' (S. Paige Baty, *American Monroe*) due in no small part to the dedication of the engaged, active fan community that endeavours to further her legacy and preserve her memory, as explored in *Fan Phenomena: Marilyn Monroe*.

MM fans' passionate devotion to their idol is documented in Laurent Morlet's television documentary *With Her* (2012). *Le Secret de la Dernière Malle de Marilyn/Unclaimed Baggage: The Unrevealed Story of Marilyn's Last Trunk* (Antoine Robin and Nan, January 2014)[3] explores Marilyn fans' determination to acquire as many of her possessions as

Introduction
Marcelline Block

Fig. 2: This bench, inscribed
with 'In Remembrance of
Marilyn Monroe From Her
Many Fans,' is situated near
Marilyn's crypt at Westwood
Village Memorial Park Cem-
etery. (© Jackie Craig).

possible, as she 'is one of the few true goddesses of the cinema, able to
confer the blessing of long life and special value on everything she may
have touched, from dresses to teapots' and other memorabilia (Richard B. Woodward, 'Iconomania'; see also Ange Webb's chapter in this
book about the Blonde Bombshell's dresses).[4]

Prominent Marilyn fans/collectors often publish their writing online and in print.
They lecture, give interviews, hold public appearances and exhibit their personal Mari-
lyn collections, including fans Gianandrea Colombo, Jackie Craig, Scott Fortner, Marijane Gray, Tara Hanks, Melinda Mason and Mary Sims, who are featured in this volume.
Along with presenting these fans' words, images and memorabilia in the following
pages, as well as those of professional Marilyn impersonators Deborah Bakker ('Debra
Monroe'), Susan Griffiths and Suzie Kennedy, the chapters of *Fan Phenomena: Marilyn
Monroe* engage with various aspects of MM fandom – such as MM's famous outfits; Marilyn lookalikes; the weeklong commemoration of Marilyn for the 50th memorial in 2012;
Marilyn's posthumous presence on screens big (*My Week with Marilyn* [Simon Curtis,
2011]), small (*Smash* [Theresa Rebeck, NBC, 2012–13]) and computer (YouTube) – and
her legacy for fans, critics, scholars and popular culture enthusiasts.

The loyalty of Marilyn's fans is addressed in this volume, which also considers her im-
pact/influence upon fashion, film, media/new media and cultural studies, among other
fields. Situated at their intersection with fan studies, a significant dialogue in *Fan Phenomena: Marilyn Monroe* occurs between fans who preserve her memory and writers,
critics and scholars who analyze her persona and interpret its significance.

Fans interviewed in this volume include members of the Immortal Marilyn Fan Club.
According to Mark Duffett, 'the network of individuals who run the Immortal Marilyn
club do not just put their energies into creating a website. They hold pilgrimages to
Hollywood, make and upload their own videos, write articles, create wallpapers, hold
memorial services, raise charity donations, review books, sketch pictures and much
more' (*Understanding Fandom*). In *Fan Phenomena: Marilyn Monroe*, fan interviewees
involved with Immortal Marilyn include the club's owner Mary Sims, who discusses Immortal Marilyn's initiatives such as placing flowers on Marilyn's crypt four times a year
and distributing holiday gifts to children at Hollygrove, the orphanage where Marilyn
had been placed as a child (then called the Los Angeles Orphans Home). Norma Jeane,
when entrusted to this orphanage, would watch, from her window, the RKO Radio Pictures neon sign, while fantasizing of becoming a star (as recalled by her one-time room-
mate, Shelley Winters, in the second volume of her 1989 memoir, *Shelley II: The Middle
of My Century*).

Along with their active engagement with the politics of mourning and memory, and
the commemoration of Marilyn's life, career and passing, a primary element of MM
fandom, as expressed by fans interviewed herewith, is a sense of belonging. Henry
Jenkins asserts that fan culture 'is responsive to the needs that draw its members to

Fig. 3: Family Circle magazine (April, 26, 1946) - the first solo American cover appearance of Marilyn Monroe (as Norma Jeane Dougherty) (© Private Collection Gianandrea Colombo)

Fig. 4: 'Marilyn Geek' Melinda Mason on her wedding day in Las Vegas, 1 June 2010 (the date chosen as a tribute to Marilyn Monroe's birthday, 1 June 1926). Mason is pictured with her two bridesmaids, the world famous Marilyn Monroe impersonators Susan Griffiths and Suzie Kennedy, both of whom are interviewed in Fan Phenomena: Marilyn Monroe (© Melinda Mason).

commercial entertainment, most especially the desire for affiliation, friendship, community' (*Textual Poachers*). As Marijane Gray states in her interview in this volume, Marilyn fandom leads to 'friendships that have deepened far beyond our love of Marilyn [...] we become family'. Milestones in many fans' lives are intertwined with Marilyn's: 'Marilyn Geek' Melinda Mason held her wedding on Marilyn's birthday (1 June); Mason's bridesmaids were world-renowned MM impersonators Susan Griffiths and Suzie Kennedy (see their interviews and photos herewith). Fans remain connected with Marilyn throughout their lives and struggles, and even in death: Ross McNaughton, an Australian member of the fan community for nearly fifty years, was offered love and support by Marilyn fans while he was fighting leukemia. Unfortunately, he succumbed on 3 April 2013; in his honour, MM fans raised funds for a memorial plaque bearing his name to be placed near Marilyn's crypt at Westwood Cemetery.

Thousands of books have been written about Marilyn, far more than about 'any other female [celebrity] over the past century' (Rollyson, *Marilyn Monroe: A Life of the Actress*). In *The Many Lives of Marilyn Monroe*, Sarah Churchwell asserts, 'Marilyn is like other pop icons in prompting adoration from fans' yet 'she is unique in being [...] sufficiently interesting for highbrow writers to devote' texts, in whole or in part, to her. In other words, 'everybody but Marlon Brando has talked or written about Marilyn Monroe' (Clara Juncker, *Circling Marilyn*). [5] Several recent publications about Marilyn include Carl Rollyson's revised and updated version of his 1986 *Marilyn Monroe: A Life of the Actress* and his *Marilyn Monroe Day by Day: A Timeline of People, Places, Events*, as well as Jacqueline Rose's Women in Dark Times, among others.

The outpouring of literary production about Marilyn recalls how she 'was a literate woman who enjoyed reading Tolstoy and Dostoevsky, but the flatland nature of her ditzy blonde icon was not complex enough to allow room for this side of her personality to surface into public view' (John David Ebert, *Dead Celebrities, Living Icons*) - although she was famously photographed reading James Joyce's *Ulysses* (1922) and was married, from 1956-1961, to a major American playwright, Arthur Miller. Her 'library contained four hundred books', including works by Beckett, Dostoyevsky, Hemingway, Kerouac, Milton and Whitman (Bernard Comment and Stanley Buchthal, *Fragments*) as well as 'works on psychology and physiology [...] copies of Mabel Elsworth Todd's *The Thinking Body*, as well as an edition of Freud's letters on her bedside table' (Rollyson, *A Life of the Actress*). Moreover, 'as soon as Marilyn signed her [Columbia Pictures] contract, she went to a Hollywood bookstore to open a charge account' (Susan Doll, 'Marilyn Monroe Signs with Columbia Pictures'). In Joyce Carol Oates's short story 'Three Girls', an in-

Introduction
Marcelline Block

cognito Marilyn, browsing in New York City's iconic Strand bookstore, is described as follows: 'you could see that this individual was a reader.' Fraser Penney, a Marilyn fan with an extensive personal library of Marilyn-centric works, has reviewed books for the *Immortal Marilyn* website since 2008. When it comes to books about Marilyn, he asks and answers his own question:

– Can we ever have enough?
– Well, I can't. ('Immortal Marilyn's January 2008 Book of the Month')

Not only are Marilyn fans such as Penney devoted to reading and reviewing the massive corpus of texts treating Marilyn, but also, as members of Marilyn's fandom often are or become authors themselves, *Fan Phenomena: Marilyn Monroe* features an excerpt from fan-author Tara Hanks's *The MMM Girl: Marilyn Monroe, by Herself...* (UKA Press, 2007). Here Hanks recreates three of Marilyn's iconic photo shoots: Andre de Dienes at Tobey Beach, 1949; Richard Avedon's 'Fabled Enchantresses' for *Life* magazine (1958) – in which Marilyn incarnated Theda Bara, Clara Bow, Marlene Dietrich and Lillian Russell –; and George Barris's Santa Monica Beach photos in July 1962, a month before her death.

The excerpt from Tara Hanks's *The MMM Girl* and Scott Fortner's text about the 50th memorial tribute to Marilyn support Henry Jenkins's claim that 'all fans are potential writers whose talents need to be discovered, nurtured, and promoted and who may be able to make a contribution [...] to the cultural wealth of the larger community' (*Textual Poachers*). Indeed, the input and contribution of fans are often acknowledged/cited in works of Marilyn scholarship.[6]

Along with the plethora of literature about Marilyn, new/social media fan tributes proliferate, including websites (personal/fan club), blogs, Tumblrs and Facebook groups. According to Kelvin Eng Yong Low, 'websites that commemorate her work and life [show] how such a cyber platform can draw together collective memory via virtual communities, akin to Anderson's (1983) imagined community' ('Memories in Context via Cyber Reminiscing'). ThisisMarilyn.com, 'the first and only social network specifically designed for the devoted fans and collectors of Marilyn Monroe's lifetime of work', was launched on 1 June 2009, on what 'would have been her eighty-third birthday' (ThisisMarilyn.com). ThisisMarilyn.com endorses Jenkins's claim that 'fandom functions as an alternative social community' and recalls that for Kelvin Eng Yong Low, writing in 2003, years before the advent of ThisisMarilyn.com:

there exists a virtual community out there, where the members, coming from all walks of life, are simultaneously remembering Marilyn...Through this, one does not remember as an isolated individual, but rather, as a social being who shares memory collectively via the cyber landscape. ('Memories in Context via Cyber Reminiscing')

Fig. 5: Marilyn fan Jim
Parson with Seward Johnson's
'Forever Marilyn' statue, April
2013, Palm Springs, CA (©
Jim Parson).

Marilyn Monroe's presence on YouTube, a form of the 'hyper-real spectacle of the celebrity's posthumous (re)incarnation [which is] eternally recreated and reproduced in the public eye' (Marcelline Block, 'Poor Little Rich Dead'), is treated by Louise Elali and Catalina Vázquez in their chapter in this volume, 'Timeless Stars and New Spotlights: Looking for Marilyn Monroe on YouTube'.

'We reassemble her, recollect her, resurrect her [...] we worship Marilyn in the way we have come to worship in late twentieth-century America: we reproduce her' (S. Paige Baty, *American Monroe*), recalling Walter Benjamin's essay 'The Work of Art in the Age of Mechanical Reproducibility' (1936). Marilyn's countless posthumous appearances in works of art include Andy Warhol's iconic silkscreens; the portrait of Marilyn by British artist Claire Milner made out of 65,000 Swarovski Crystals, and Seward Johnson's 25-foot-tall 'Forever Marilyn' statue recreating Marilyn's iconic pose (wearing the white dress designed by William Travilla) in *The Seven Year Itch* (Billy Wilder, 1955). 'Forever Marilyn' is featured throughout this volume in photos taken by Marilyn fans including Jackie Craig, Leah Peterson, Jim Parson and Kara Pugh who pose with it. On September 15, 2014, the hair care label Sexy Hair – whose logo is Marilyn's face – commemorated the 60th anniversary of the filming of this scene during which Marilyn's white dress billows in the air as she stands on a subway grate on Manhattan's Lexington Avenue and 52nd street by inviting fans to imitate her pose at this very location as part of the '#mymarilynmoment' social media campaign.

Fig. 6: The Adelphi Theatre
on London's West End when
Marilyn! The Musical (dir.
Frank Muller), starring
Stephanie Lawrence, was
performed there in 1983.
(© Jackie Craig).

Homages and references to Marilyn also abound in music – pop, country, rap, opera, shows on Broadway and on London's West End as well as the fictitious Marilyn Broadway musical *Bombshell*, the *mise en abyme* of the television series *Smash*, addressed elsewhere in this volume by Raquel Crisóstomo – and in the works and music videos of entertainers who express their own Marilyn fandom when imitating and/or paying tribute to her, ensuring her posthumous longevity.

As Clara Juncker observes, 'Marilyn impersonated Mae West, Betty Grable, Jean Harlow, and especially Marilyn Monroe [...] [turning] "Marilyn" on and off depending on mood and circumstance' (*Circling Marilyn*), recalling the claim that 'as Marilyn performed herself, others may now perform themselves as versions of the icon' (S. Paige Baty, *American Monroe*): performers including Christina Aguilera, Pamela Anderson, Mariah Carey, Amanda Lepore, Madonna, Nicki Minaj, Brianna Perry, Lana Del Rey and Britney Spears, along with the roster of actresses who, over the years, have portrayed Marilyn on the big and/or small screens, such as Michelle Williams, who won a Golden Globe for playing MM in *My Week with Marilyn* (discussed by Zachary Ingle in this volume) and Megan Hilty, Katharine McPhee and Uma Thurman in *Smash*, examined herewith by Raquel Crisóstomo. Singers, actresses, entertainers and models such as Loni

Introduction
Marcelline Block

Anderson, Beyoncé, Lady Gaga, Rachel Hunter, Scarlett Johansson, Angelina Jolie, Nicole Kidman, Lindsay Lohan, Jennifer Lopez, Kylie Minogue, Kate Moss, Gwyneth Paltrow, Andreja Pejic, Rihanna, Jessica Simpson, Gwen Stefani and Anna Nicole Smith, among others, have (re)appropriated Marilyn's style in contexts including performances, magazine covers, photo shoots, advertisements, products such as Paris Hilton's 'Tease' fragrance, and, in the case of James Franco, wearing Marilyn drag during a segment when he co-hosted the 83rd Academy Awards ceremony (2011). Upcoming interpretations of Marilyn in film and television include Andrew Dominik's big-screen adaptation of Joyce Carol Oates's *Blonde* (scheduled for release in 2016) starring Jessica Chastain and Lifetime's 2015 *Marilyn* with Kelli Garner in the titular role.

In the video for her song 'Don't Forget About Us' (2005), Mariah Carey, a lifelong MM fan, recreates the iconic swimming pool footage of Marilyn from her final (unfinished) film, *Something's Got to Give* (George Cukor, 1962). Carey further demonstrated the extent of her fandom by naming one of her twins, daughter Monroe Cannon (b. 2011)[7], after Marilyn, and also purchasing Marilyn's legendary white baby grand piano, the subject of *Smash*'s eponymous song 'Second-Hand White Baby Grand' (see Raquel Crisóstomo's chapter 'Marilyn is a *Smash*'). In a June 2014 interview with *Out*, Carey stated that Marilyn 'paved the way for women in Hollywood [...] every single woman owes something to her for that, whether they agree with her image or not' (Rebecca McAtee, *E! Online*).

And that image 'lives (on) as refrigerator magnet, coffee cup, earrings, diary cover, poster girl [...] whichever Marilyn one prefers' (Clara Juncker, 'Marketing Marilyn'). The manifold instances of the continuous reproduction of Marilyn's image for public consumption, which fuels fan worship, include the following: her cartoon avatar 'Mini Marilyn', icon of the eponymous brand aimed toward girls aged 8–16; her image displayed on haute couture items such as Dolce and Gabbana gowns and the more budget-friendly Macy's Marilyn Monroe line of clothing; displaying her famous sayings (known as 'Marilynisms' or 'Monroeisms') and photos on the chocolates, mints and gummies comprising the 'Marilyn Monroe' line of sweets at US confectionary It's Sugar, whose very name alludes to her iconic character Sugar Kane's line 'It's me, Sugar' in *Some Like It Hot* (Billy Wilder, 1959); fans and collectors spending large sums of money at auction for dresses owned/worn by Marilyn, as examined by Ange Webb in her chapter, 'Marilyn Monroe's Dresses' or the professional lookalike/tribute artists who physically embody her – such as the MM impersonators played on-screen by Bridget Fonda in *Finding Graceland* (David Winkler, 1998) and Samantha Morton in *Mister Lonely* (Harmony Korine, 2007) – discussed by Ross Sloan in his chapter 'Lipstick Thespians: Being Marilyn Monroe after 5 August 1962', whose work he likens to gravedigging... Alas, poor Marilyn!

Indeed, upon dying, major popular culture figures such as Marilyn, come to, as previously discussed in a different context,

Fig. 7: Gianandrea Colombo, coordinator of the Marilyn Monroe Italia fan club, with professional Marilyn Monroe lookalikes Memory Monroe and Holly Beavon, August 2012, Hollywood (CA) (© Gianandrea Colombo).

represent something greater than their own fame, or even themselves. They are 'Lacanian entities of unreachable plenitude' (Szaniawski), substitutes for deities and idols in previous historical eras as they are 'a modern electronic equivalent of saints' (Ebert) of the 'secular religion' of fame (Braudy). (Marcelline Block, 'Poor Little Rich Dead')

recalling that for Clara Juncker, 'part oracle and part disciple [...] the Marilyn impersonator acknowledges the fluid boundaries between stars and religious figures that make fans seek them out' (*Circling Marilyn*).

Moreover, after 'leaving this world, these celebrities are granted not just immortality, but also soulful commemoration and some kindly attention' (Marcelline Block, 'Poor Little Rich Dead'). One such commemoration to Marilyn is the annual memorial in her honour, which, since 1982, has been held by the Marilyn Remembered Fan Club (see Scott Fortner's chapter herewith).

As demonstrated by the interdisciplinary nature of this volume, there is much promising possibility for research and scholarship in the domain of Marilyn Monroe fandom. This book is infused with Marilyn's spirit: she recognized and acknowledged her debt to her audience and viewership when she stated that 'the people' – and not the film industry – had elevated her to stardom (Richard Meryman, *Life*, 1962).[8] In recognition of MM fans' importance to her career and legacy, *Fan Phenomena: Marilyn Monroe* pays tribute to the Marilyn Monroe fandom community.

notes

1. Her birth certificate incorrectly gives her last name as "Mortenson" rather than "Mortensen."

2. Raquel Crisóstomo's chapter about *Smash* primarily focuses on *Smash*'s first season, since according to showrunner Joshua Safran, the second season featured 'less Marilyn' as it 'introduced Hit List, a separate musical' (interview with Denise Martin of Vulture.com/*New York Magazine*, 4 February 2013).

3. I am indebted to Gabriel Solomons, series editor of *Fan Phenomena*, for this reference.

4. For further examination of how individuals, including MM fans, relate to/engage with/find meaning from a dress once owned/worn by Marilyn, see Yury Toroptsov's *Marilyn and I* (Paris: Verlhac, 2011).

5. However, Marlon Brando did write about Marilyn in his memoir *Songs My Mother Taught Me* (1994), including details about their romantic relationship and subsequent friendship, as well as firmly stating his belief that Marilyn was murdered: Brando claims to have spoken with her by phone several days prior to her death, and that she was not suicidal. Incidentally, in terms of onomastics it is worth noting that the two first names 'Marilyn' and 'Marlon' contain similarities: the same first and last letter; five letters in common: M, A, R, L, N (which includes the first and last letters of both names); the same consonants as well as identical first syllables ('Mar'): it almost looks as if 'Marilyn'

Introduction
Marcelline Block

could be the feminine counterpart of 'Marlon'. At this juncture, we should note that Marlon Brando was born 'Marlon' whereas 'Marilyn Monroe' was a stage name given to her by Ben Lyon at Twentieth Century Fox, who bestowed this name upon Norma Jeane in her early days as an actress. Note that Lyon re-named Norma Jeane 'Marilyn' after the 1920s actress Marilyn Miller (itself a stage name, as she was born Mary Ellen Reynolds); later on, after marrying playwright and author Arthur Miller, Marilyn Monroe was to become Marilyn Monroe Miller. Both Marilyns share a similar fate of dying in their mid-thirties: Marilyn Miller from complications of a surgery following a nasal infection at age 37 in 1936; while Marilyn Monroe died at age 36, officially from 'acute barbiturate poisoning'.

6. For example, Lois Banner partially dedicates her 2012 book *Marilyn: The Passion and the Paradox*, to Greg Schreiner, one of the leading figures of Marilyn fandom. See Greg Schreiner's The Marilyn Monroe Site, http://www.themarilynmonroesite.com/.

7. Whereas singer Brian Hugh Warner (b. 1969) is better known by his stage name 'Marilyn Manson' which he derived from combining the names Marilyn Monroe and Charles Manson: in Marilyn Manson's words, 'Marilyn Monroe wasn't even her real name, Charles Manson isn't his real name, and now, I'm taking that to be my real name. But what's real? You can't find the truth, you just pick the lie you like the best.'

8. During her lifetime, Marilyn received tens of thousands of fan letters, far more than her contemporary actors: 'by 1954, Marilyn was receiving as many as twenty-thousand fan letters a week, setting a new record among film stars' (Lois Banner, MM-Personal).

GO FURTHER

Books
American Monroe: The Making of a Body Politic
S. Paige Baty
(Berkeley: University of California Press, 1995)

Circling Marilyn: Text Body Performance
Clara Juncker
(Odense: University Press of Southern Denmark, 2010)

Dead Celebrities, Living Icons: Tragedy and Fame in the Age of the Multimedia Superstar
John David Ebert
(Santa Barbara, CA: Praeger, 2010)

Fragments: Poems, Intimate Notes, Letters
Marilyn Monroe, with Bernard Comment (ed.) and Stanley Buchthal (narr.)
(New York: Farrar, Straus & Giroux, 2010)

The Immortal Marilyn: The Depiction of an Icon
John De Vito and Frank Tropea
(Lanham, MD: Scarecrow Press, 2006)

The Many Lives of Marilyn Monroe
Sarah Churchwell
(New York: Henry Holt and Company, 2004)

Marilyn: The Passion and the Paradox
Lois Banner
(New York: Bloomsbury, 2012)

Marilyn Monroe: A Life of the Actress, Revised and Updated
Carl Rollyson
(University Press of Mississippi, 2014)

MM-Personal: From the Private Archive of Marilyn Monroe
Lois Banner
(New York: Abrams, 2010)

Introduction
Marcelline Block

Shelley II: The Middle of My Century
Shelley Winters
(New York: Simon and Schuster, 1989)

Songs my Mother Taught Me
Marlon Brando, with Robert Lindsey
(New York: Random House, 1994)

Textual Poachers: Television Fans and Participatory Culture
Henry Jenkins
(New York: Routledge, 2013; 2nd edn)

Understanding Fandom: An Introduction to the Study of Media Fan Culture
Mark Duffett
(Bloomsbury Academic, 2013)

Book Chapters
'Iconomania: Sex, Death, Photography, and the Myth of Marilyn Monroe'
Richard B. Woodward In Yona Zeldis McDonough (ed.). *All of the Available Light: A Marilyn Monroe Reader* (New York: Touchstone Books, 2002, e-book version), 10-34.

'Marketing Marilyn'
Clara Juncker
In Clara Juncker and Russell Duncan (eds). *Trading Cultures: Nationalism and Globalization in American Studies* Vol. 2: *Angles on the English-Speaking World* (Odense: University of Copenhagen, 2002), pp. 37-50.

'Poor Little Rich Dead: Michael Jackson's Moonwalk through the Pharmaco-Narco Netherworld and Other Tales of Celebrity Death and Inequality'
Marcelline Block
In Marcelline Block and Christina Staudt (eds). *Unequal Before Death* (Newcastle, UK: Cambridge Scholars Press, 2012), pp. 149-92.

Short Stories
'Three Girls'
Joyce Carol Oates
In Joyce Carol Oates, *I Am No One You Know: And Other Stories* (HarperCollins, 2009; e-book version)

Articles
'An Iconic Star for an Iconic Brand: Marilyn Monroe is the Face of Max Factor Cosmetics!'
Marianne Mychaskiw
InStyle.com. 6 January 2015, http://news.instyle.com/2015/01/06/an-iconic-star-for-an-iconic-brand-marilyn-monroe-is-the-face-of-max-factor-cosmetics/.

'Gentlemen Prefer Blondes! Marilyn Monroe Voted Most Glamorous Star of All Time'
Sarah Barns
The Express. 13 June 2014, http://www.express.co.uk/life-style/style/482215/Marilyn-Monroe-and-Sean-Connery-voted-most-glamorous-stars.

'How *Smash* Learned to Stop Worrying and Love the Hate-Watchers'
Denise Martin
Vulture.com. 4 February 2013, http://www.vulture.com/2013/02/how-ismashi-learned-to-love-the-hate-watchers.html.

'Jessica Chastain to Play Marilyn Monroe in Andrew Dominik's *Blonde*'
Jeff Sneider
TheWrap.com. 22 April 2014, http://www.thewrap.com/jessica-chastain-play-marilyn-monroe-andrew-dominik-blonde-brad-pitt-plan-b/

'Kelli Garner to Play Marilyn Monroe in Lifetime Miniseries'
Nellie Andreeva
Deadline.com. 27 October 2014, http://deadline.com/2014/10/kelli-garner-cast-marilyn-monroe-marilyn-lifetime-miniseries-863139/.

'Mariah Carey, 44, Is "Eternally 12-Years-Old": Why Her *Out* Interview Shows She Really Is a Tween!'
Rebecca McAtee. *E! Online*, 25 June 2014, http://www.eonline.com/news/554244/mariah-carey-44-is-eternally-12-years-old-why-her-out-interview-shows-she-really-is-a-tween.

'Marilyn Monroe Signs with Columbia Pictures.' Susan Doll (n.d.), http://entertainment.howstuffworks.com/marilyn-monroe-early-career2.htm.

'Memories in Context via Cyber Reminiscing: The Case of Marilyn Monroe'
Kelvin Eng Yong Low
The Qualitative Report. 8: 4 (2003), pp. 607–23.

Introduction
Marcelline Block

Bibliography
Marilyn Monroe: Una bibliografia
Frederic Cabanas
(Barcelona: Ixiz llibres, 1992)

Interview
'Marilyn Monroe Lets Her Hair Down About Being Famous: 'Fame My Go By and So Long, I've Had You'...An Interview.'
Richard Meryman
Life. 3 August 1962.

Social Media
ThisisMarilyn.com: http://www.thisismarilyn.com

Book Review
'Immortal Marilyn's January 2008 Book of the Month'
Fraser Penney. Immortal Marilyn, 25 June 2014, *http://immortalmarilyn.com/ BOTMMmmGirl.html*

Exhibits:
'Marilyn: The Lost Photographs of a Hollywood Star', travelling exhibit by Limited Runs (Pierre Vudrag, curator): *http://www.limitedruns.com/blog/movie/marilyn-the-lost-photographs-of-a-hollywood-star/*

Music Videos:
Mariah Carey, 'Don't Forget About Us,' dir. Paul Hunter (The Island Def Jam Music Group, 2005).
[See: *https://www.youtube.com/watch?v=8tZkzL4j3BU*]

Films:
Mister Lonely, Harmony Korine, dir. (France: Love Streams Productions/An O'SALVATION Production, 2007).

Products:
Marilyn Monroe Candy, an It's Sugar Exclusive:
http://www.itsugar.com/candy/marilyn-monroe-candy.html

'THEY'VE TRIED TO
MANUFACTURE OTHER
MARILYN MONROES AND
THEY WILL UNDOUBTEDLY
KEEP TRYING.
BUT IT WON'T WORK.
SHE WAS AN ORIGINAL.'

BILLY WILDER,
DIRECTOR OF *SOME LIKE IT HOT*

Chapter
1

Timeless Stars and New Spotlights: Looking for Marilyn Monroe on YouTube

Louise Elali and Catalina Vázquez

→ **I've never fooled anyone. I've let people fool themselves. They didn't bother to find out who and what I was. Instead they would invent a character for me. I wouldn't argue with them. They were obviously loving somebody I wasn't.**
– Marilyn Monroe

Fig. 1: 'US TV series Smash's 'duelling Marilyns,' Ivy Lynn (Megan Hilty) and Karen Cartwright (Katharine McPhee) (© Madwoman in the Attic)

In 2006, PBS aired a Marilyn Monroe tribute entitled *Marilyn Monroe: Still Life* (dir. Gail Levin), which featured American feminist icon Gloria Steinem, who, in her 1986 essay 'The Woman Who Will Not Die', wrote that,

It has been nearly a quarter of a century since the death of a minor American actress named Marilyn Monroe [...] If you add her years of movie stardom to the years since her death, Marilyn Monroe has been a part of our lives and imaginations for nearly four decades. That's a very long time for one celebrity to survive in a throwaway culture [...] As I write this, she is still better known than most living movie stars, most world leaders, and most television personalities.

More recently, University of Southern California Professor Emerita Lois W. Banner, author of *MM-Personal: From the Private Archive of Marilyn Monroe* (2010) as well as *Marilyn: The Passion and the Paradox* (2012), wrote an opinion piece in the 5 August 2012 edition of the *Los Angeles Times*, which marked the 50th anniversary of Marilyn's death:

Why is Marilyn Monroe still an American icon 50 years after her death? She is endlessly analyzed in films and biographies; her image appears on T-shirts and posters; her popularity is reflected in the 52,000 Marilyn-related items for sale on EBay. My USC students, fixated on contemporary pop culture, know little about 1950s Hollywood stars, except for Monroe. Like everyone else, they puzzle over her death, respond to her beauty, and recognize her paradoxes: the ur-blond child-woman, the virgin-whore of the Western imagination.

Although it might be hard to explain why, it is rather easy to observe that Marilyn's figure is still as effervescent and inspiring as it has ever been, even more than half a century after her death. In a culture where celebrities are 'the flavour of the week' – they quickly gain exposure, become over-exposed and fade away – Marilyn seems to be more popular than ever, and interest in her persona has only increased. She is often featured in an array of mass media productions, from television shows like NBC's *Smash* (Theresa Rebeck, 2012-13) and its 'duelling Marilyns' – as the press referred to Ivy Lynn (Megan Hilty) and Karen Cartwright (Katharine McPhee), the show's characters competing to play Marilyn in a Broadway musical based on her life – to Michelle Williams's lauded and award-winning portrayal of the star in the film *My Week with Marilyn* (Simon Curtis, 2011), to countless books about her life [Editor's note: see the chapters elsewhere in this volume about *Smash* and *My Week with Marilyn*]. The test of time has proven that Marilyn Monroe is a lasting cultural icon as the quintessential sex symbol

Timeless Stars and New Spotlights:
Looking for Marilyn Monroe on YouTube
Louise Elali and Catalina Vázquez

and pop culture motif.

Indeed, Marilyn remains a vibrant presence in the world's collective memory to this day. However, what does she truly represent? While alive, Monroe longed to be seen as a serious actress, but she struggled with the reality that many people only saw her as a sex symbol. One of her famous quotes describes her thoughts on this matter: 'Some people have been unkind. If I say I want to grow as an actress, they look at my figure. If I say I want to develop, to learn my craft, they laugh. Somehow they don't expect me to be serious about my work.'

While she was indeed a successful and highly recognized actress, it seems she felt that her on-screen roles did not match her off-screen strength and individuality. Although she often played the stereotypical dumb blonde in comedy films, she ultimately wanted to be accepted as a serious artist, taking steps like moving to New York so she could participate in classes on the Method, a highly disciplined acting technique based on the great Russian director Constantin Stanislavski. In her final interview, Marilyn pleaded: 'Please don't make me a joke. End the interview with what I believe. I don't mind making jokes, but I don't want to look like one [...] I want to be an artist, an actress with integrity.'

Although biographies state that Marilyn herself never managed to change the public's perception of her while she was alive, she now has many fans that defend both her on-screen and off-screen personalities with incredible fervour, which piqued our curiosity. We wanted to find out if these fans have managed to do the very thing that Marilyn could not accomplish during her lifetime: are they indeed turning Marilyn's iconic sex symbol image into that of a serious actress? In order to answer this question, we decided to take a look at the 'Marilyn Monroe' videos posted on YouTube. More specifically, we wanted to see what Marilyn-related content is being produced and reproduced these days, and equally as important, what that means for the star's time-honoured iconic image.

YouTube is the perfect social media platform to use in addressing such a socially complex query. Not only is it currently the third most visited site in the world (coming in just after Facebook and Google), but this social media-based website seriously gives way to a growing bottom-up, user-generated approach to creating stardom, since it is guided by 'prosumption' – a word used to describe the users' role in social media platforms by combining 'production' and 'consumption'. On the other hand, it still incorporates the long-standing Hollywood star system. In this newer and visual space, Hollywood idols reclaim their status as timeless icons that are found, re-found, re-introduced and re-created within this cluster of participant-led content.

Like Marilyn Monroe herself, the YouTube platform came from left field, unexpected but explosive, and, like the beloved actress that demanded and gained attention from people all over the world, this social media tool we have all come to know – and in many ways, depend upon – has requested and received participation from all kinds of people.

Kiss Marilyn Monroe

Fig. 2: 'According to Cesar Suero in Forbes.com, "for every
YouTube visitor in high school
there is another one who is
old enough to remember
Marilyn Monroe, whose star
still shines brightly on the
video-sharing Web site." (©
John Brecher/MSNBC.com)

It has become truly significant in the way we communicate in our society. Within this organized chaos that is actually video sharing led by prosumers, we dig for the standing of our beloved Hollywood star in our collective memory.

Collective memory is a shared pool of information held in the memories of a group. In the 2011 article 'Collective Memory and Video-sharing in the Internet', Segah Sak explains that collective memory can be described as based upon the following six premises:

1. Processual, because it is 'a transforming, unfolding and changing process'
2. Unpredictable, for it does not follow a linear or rational logic
3. Partial, as it engages a range of fragments from diverse histories
4. Usable, since it can facilitate the connections that are necessary for the production of meanings
5. Particular and universal, considering that it can characterize both a particular past occurrence for a specific group and a universal connotation for another
6. Material, as it exists out in the world, and not only in our minds

In fact, communication scholars have been exploring the relationship between the Internet in general – and YouTube in particular – and collective memory for some time now. In an essay published in the 2011 book *Navigating Landscapes of Mediated Memory*, Valentina Gueorguieva explains how 'collective memory' becomes 'online collective memory' when paired with the Internet (and especially with YouTube). In new media, memory is constructed in a process of meaning-making while searching, selecting and rearranging parts, which is a process where the user is guided by his or her emotions. If memory is a way to conserve history, digital media not only puts forward new potential for preserving and representing the past, but also, at the same time, it lets the individual express creativity and expressivity in their own interpretations and remixes of historical records, which are then shared with not only friends but possibly many anonymous fellow users. This is the defining characteristic of new media: the Internet (and more specifically, YouTube) permits a more democratic prosumer approach that combines official discourses and mediated memory-making. The author also reminds us that 'we no longer watch film or TV, we watch databases'. In this context, YouTube becomes an archive of information that the user manipulates based on the database: he or she can search, view, navigate, comment, create lists or add content, appropriate and remix digital material into new compilations.

In other words, collective memory refers to the shared knowledge and perceptions of any group of people, and online collective memory adds on the contemporary context created by the Internet. In our study, these concepts create a bridge between the

Timeless Stars and New Spotlights:
Looking for Marilyn Monroe on YouTube
Louise Elali and Catalina Vázquez

user-generated videos posted on YouTube and representations of Marilyn Monroe. After all, we intend to find out whether the actress's overall image is shifting in the public eye (which would be mirrored in the YouTube videos shared by the prosumers), and, consequently, collective memory.

Fig. 3: A promotion for the video of Brianna Perry's song, 'Marilyn Monroe' (©Atlantic Records)

Therefore, in order to approach these concepts in a more concrete manner, we decided to focus on Monroe's presence on YouTube. The pop icon and quintessential sex symbol was an obvious choice for a case study, since her stardom has carried over for decades and her image is consequently firmly cemented in collective memory. As a result, our research question became: do YouTube representations of Marilyn Monroe play into or move away from the Hollywood narratives in which she was originally placed?

The next step was, then, to perform a simple YouTube search for 'Marilyn Monroe'. As an anonymous user (as in 'not logged in'), we set the language to 'English (US)' and picked 'Worldwide' on the location menu as well as turned off the safety system. The results were ordered by relevance.

Under these parameters, 70 per cent of the videos brought forward consisted in simple repostings of movie scenes from Marilyn Monroe's film career such as Marilyn's performance of the song 'I Wanna Be Loved by You' (Herbert Stothart and Bert Kalmar, 1928) in the movie *Some Like It Hot* (Billy Wilder, 1959), an unmistakable favourite (repeated three times in the twenty videos, with 'Diamonds Are a Girl's Best Friend' [Jule Styne and Leo Robin, 1949] from Howard Hawks's 1953 film *Gentlemen Prefer Blondes* as a close second); footage of the actress herself (her iconic rendition of 'Happy Birthday Mr. President' appeared three times in the sample, although from different angles), or diverse parts of the 2001 television documentary entitled *Marilyn: The Final Days* (dir. Patty Ivins), which means that, on this website, original presentations of the actress take precedence over user-generated representations. Since our initial intentions were to analyse how the performer is recaptured in the YouTube canon by its users, we decided to add an extra filter we called 'variation'. Therefore, we excluded videos that showed solely material performed by Marilyn Monroe herself, including scenes from movies, performances, and tribute-like photomontages set to one of her songs.

As a result, the data collection was performed again, and we created a new sample of twenty videos, gathered in the last week of April 2012. The videos were analysed on the basis of:

- Basic Video Data: recording each video's metadata, namely, title, date posted, total views, number of comments, likes and dislikes, category and tags
- User Info/Posting Context: looking at the user's declared country and age
- Audio: whether the video's audio was exclusively a song or spoken language, or was composed of a mix of the two
- Production Quality: establishing if the content was generated by the user (or, better yet, prosumer) or a simple copy of a professionally created production

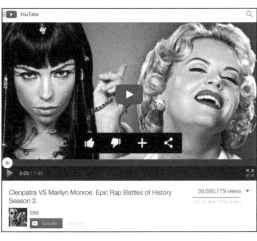

• Original Content: we registered if and how Marilyn herself was present in the video, i.e. in a visual manner (moving or still image), in an audible manner (through her voice, either in a song or a dialogue), both or none
• Reference: if Marilyn herself was not part of the video, how did the piece convey the actress? The options were through visual elements (clothing, accessories, blonde hair, mole, make-up, among others), by name, or in another unpredicted manner

Fig. 4: 'Epic Rap Battles of History: Cleopatra vs. Marilyn Monroe', YouTube, 7 May 2012 (© ERB)

Fig. 5: MAC's Marilyn Monroe limited edition cosmetics collection, 'Holiday 2012.' (© MAC)

Overall, we found that Marilyn Monroe is still a very relevant pop culture icon, with a constant presence in collective memory. This idea is supported by the reality that 95 per cent of the videos were posted in the last six months (as of 2012), and the films were rather popular, averaging 265,645 views, 3,562 comments, 4,039 likes and 374 dislikes per item.

These results go hand in hand with the fact that 65 per cent of the videos were professionally produced for a variety of media, and, therefore, mainstream. They included music industry productions such as two songs by contemporary artists Nicki Minaj and Brianna Perry, which are not only named after Marilyn Monroe but also mention the actress in the lyrics, and an 'Epic Rap Battles of History' episode centred on a showdown between Cleopatra and Marilyn Monroe; several re-imaginations of Marilyn and/or her movies previously aired on television such as NBC's *Smash* musical numbers and episode previews, Blake Lively's re-creation of 'Diamonds Are a Girl's Best Friend' for the CW series *Gossip Girl* (Josh Safran, 2007–12); interviews with actresses such as Michelle Williams who took on the role of Marilyn along with *Broadway.com*'s piece about *Smash* actress Megan Hilty incarnating Marilyn in an Encore stage production of *Gentlemen Prefer Blondes*; other items with Marilyn-related content, like an announcement for MAC's new line of cosmetics inspired by the famous actress; and other such tributes. Only 35 per cent of the videos were considered user-generated, and those items were mostly 'how to' tutorials, explaining how to achieve Marilyn's sexy look through a specific make-up technique or hairstyle.

The most common tags provide a good overall picture of the content portrayed in the videos, since many words were related to the TV show *Smash*, including the cast's names (i.e. 'smash', 'musical', 'megan', 'hilty', 'katharine' and 'mcphee'), as well as 'michelle', 'williams', 'nicki' and 'minaj'. Other frequent words refer to appearance (i.e. 'look', 'beauty', 'cosmetics' and 'tutorial'). As a result, it is not surprising to find out that the videos were usually posted under the category of 'Entertainment', which made up 45 per cent of the sample. In addition, there was also a strong presence in the category 'How to & Style' (25 per cent).

Forty per cent of the videos analysed included 'original' content (usually pictures

Timeless Stars and New Spotlights:
Looking for Marilyn Monroe on YouTube
Louise Elali and Catalina Vázquez

of Marilyn herself in the background). The other 60 per cent, which did not include 'original' Monroe material, usually relied on name-dropping, which was a more common way of referencing the beloved actress than leaning solely on her iconic look, although both methods were often used in conjunction.

Fig. 6: 'Kandee Johnson: Marilyn Monroe's MAKE-UP' video tutorial, (YouTube, 18 October 2010) (© Kandee Johnson)

Therefore, Marilyn is referred to from new spaces of production, which are based on her name and image, and her references are popular and mainstream. A lot of the content centres on taking on her persona, either professionally, through acting in movies and television shows or 'in real life', by appropriating her looks through advanced make-up skills or particular hairdos. Consequently, much of the Marilyn content refers to a gender performance she expressed wanting to break away from during her career, with a heavy focus on image, body, good looks and sex appeal.

Based on these findings, we cannot help but wonder what are the larger implications about gender inequalities in contemporary society, issues with which Marilyn herself seems to have been preoccupied? Does the similar past and current emphasis on Monroe's sexuality imply a lack of progress in terms of structural inequalities since the time of her career? How so?

Moreover, we question the true relationship between the Internet (via YouTube) and collective memory. The scholarly implication that digital media is able to change and re-shape collective memory does not seem to play out as strongly as predicted. However, these are certainly the early stages of this technology, and this relationship can unquestionably progress and become more (or less) intrinsic over time. Consequently, although the Internet in general and YouTube in particular are seen as new influences on collective memory, capable of restructuring it because of its prosumer-centric approach, this case study hints at the possibility that these changes might be more punctual than expected, since Marilyn Monroe is kept in the same type of role she fulfilled while she was alive, even though she expressed an apparent desire (often re-affirmed by her fans) to move away from that. In spite of this, her public persona was so powerful that her image still holds similar values to what she represented decades ago. There are no signs (other than her and her fans' wishes) that this star be remembered differently or under a more dynamic interpretation any time soon.

Monroe has often been (erroneously) quoted as having said, 'Give a girl the right shoes, and she can conquer the world.' Although she did not manage to achieve her goal of changing her image, we suppose maybe she just did not own the right footwear. Could the Internet and YouTube be the new pair of pumps Marilyn Monroe was missing? Only time can tell. ●

N.B.: Some of the material in this chapter appears in Louise Elali and Catalina Vázquez's unpublished conference paper draft, 'New Memories of Old Stars: Carmen Miranda and Marilyn Monroe in the YouTube Cannon [sic],' http://www.inter-discipli-

nary.net/at-the-interface/wp-content/uploads/2012/12/elaliholpaper.pdf, presented at Hollywood and the World, *Sydney, Australia, 7–9 February 2013.*

~~~~~~~~~~

GO FURTHER

Books
Marilyn: The Passion and the Paradox
Lois Banner
(New York: Bloomsbury, 2012)

Qualitative Content Analysis in Practice
Margrit Schreier
(London: Sage, 2012)

Visual Methodologies: An Introduction to Researching with Visual Materials
Gillian Rose
(London: Sage, 2012; 3rd edn)

MM-Personal: From the Private Archive of Marilyn Monroe
Lois Banner
(New York: Abrams, 2010)

The YouTube Reader
Pelle Snickars and Patrick Vonderau (eds)
(Lithuania: Logotipas, 2009)

Time Passages: Collective Memory and American Popular Culture
George Lipsitz
(Minnesota: UMP, 2001)

Chapters
'Collective Memory and Video-sharing on the Internet'
Segah Sak
In Andreas Treske, Ulfuk Önen, Bestem Büyüm and I. Alev Degim (eds). *Image, Time and Motion: New Media Critique from Turkey, Ankara (2003–2010)* (Amsterdam: Institute of Network Cultures, 2011), pp. 94–103.
[Also available online: http://networkcultures.org/_uploads/tod/TOD%237_definitief_LQ.pdf.]

Timeless Stars and New Spotlights:
Looking for Marilyn Monroe on YouTube
Louise Elali and Catalina Vázquez

'Remixes and Appropriations of Socialist Legacy Online'
Valentina Gueorguieva
In Paul Wilson and Patrick McEntaggart (eds). *Navigating Landscapes of Mediated Memory* (Oxford, UK: Inter-Disciplinary Press, 2011).
[Also available online: http://www.inter-disciplinary.net/wp-content/uploads/2011/02/georgievadmpaper.pdf.]

Online
Articles
'Marilyn Monroe: The Eternal Shape-shifter'
Lois Banner
Los Angeles Times. 5 August 2012, http://articles.latimes.com/2012/aug/05/opinion/la-oe-0805-banner-marilyn-monroe-icon-biography-20120805.

'Rachel York, Aaron Lazar and More Join Megan Hilty in Encores! *Gentlemen Prefer Blondes*'
BWW News Desk
Broadwayworld.com. 12 April 2012, http://www.broadwayworld.com/article/Rachel-York-Aaron-Lazar-and-More-Join-Megan-Hilty-in-Encores-GENTLEMEN-PREFER-BLONDES-20120412#.UOOaFV64klI.

'The Woman Who Will Not Die'
Gloria Steinem (1986)
PBS.org. 19 July 2006, http://www.pbs.org/wnet/americanmasters/episodes/marilyn-monroe/marilyn-monroe-still-life/61/.

'YouTube Yields Video Gems for Adults, too'
Cesar Suero,
Forbes.com, 1 October 2006,
http://www.nbcnews.com/id/15067526/ns/technology_and_science-tech_and_gadgets/t/youtube-yields-video-gems-adults-too/#.U3ow9XZ8oUU

Films
Some Like It Hot, Billy Wilder, dir. (United States: Ashton Productions/The Mirisch Corporation, 1959).
Gentlemen Prefer Blondes, Howard Hawks, dir. (United States: Twentieth Century Fox, 1953).

Television
Smash, Theresa Rebeck, creator (United States: NBC, 2012–13).
Gossip Girl, Josh Safran, creator (United States: CW, 2007–12).

Marilyn: The Final Days, Patty Ivins, dir. (United States: AMC/Fox Television Productions/Prometheus Entertainment, 2001).
Marilyn Monroe: Still Life, Gail Levin, dir. (United States: Thirteen/WNET, 2006).

Songs
'Marilyn Monroe'
Nicki Minaj
In Nicki Minaj, *Pink Friday: Roman Reloaded* (Cash Money Records and Universal Republic, 2012).

'Marilyn Monroe' [Single]
Brianna Perry
(Atlantic Records, 2011)

Products
Cosmetics
M.A.C. Marilyn Monroe limited edition collection, 'Holiday 2012'.

Videos
'Epic Rap Battles of History: Cleopatra vs. Marilyn Monroe'
ERB (YouTube, 7 May 2012)
https://www.youtube.com/watch?v=vICX-6dMOuA

'Kandee Johnson: Marilyn Monroe's MAKE-UP' [Video tutorial]
Kandee Johnson (YouTube, 18 October 2010)
https://www.youtube.com/watch?v=-Dljlivw3KM.

Music Videos
Nicki Minaj
'Marilyn Monroe,' unofficial music video by YouTube user winicyuz1
https://www.youtube.com/watch?v=CCXbgGzs0YI

Brianna Perry
'Marilyn Monroe,' official music video, directed by Coodie & Chike
https://www.youtube.com/watch?v=4BzOBxQjSLM

Fan Appreciation no.1
Mary Sims, Owner of the Immortal Marilyn Fan Club Website

Fig. 1: Immortal Marilyn's Mary Sims photographed with some of the items from her Marilyn Monroe collection. (© Mary Sims)

Interview by Marcelline Block

Why, when and how did you become involved with Marilyn Monroe fandom?
I cannot remember a time not being fascinated by the subject of Marilyn Monroe. I became a serious fan/student of hers in 1988, reading Anthony Summer's book *Goddess: The Secret Lives of Marilyn Monroe* [1985]. I was to learn as I continued to read more books that there were a lot of untruths in that book. I think that only fuelled my passion to learn the 'truths', so to speak, and thus becoming a serious student of Marilyn Monroe. Before I had a computer, there was no contact with any other Marilyn fans. In 2000, I joined Yahoo! Groups in search of Marilyn Monroe fan clubs so I could meet and share my interest in Marilyn with other like-minded fans.

What is the extent of your involvement with Marilyn Monroe fandom, and which fandom communities in particular?
I am the owner of *Immortal Marilyn*. In 2003, I became the President of the Immortal Marilyn Fan Club, located in Yahoo! Groups. In 2007, the fan club part of *Immortal Marilyn* located in Yahoo! Groups was closed to concentrate solely on www.immortalmarilyn.com. The staff I had at *Immortal Marilyn* for the most part followed me and each contributes monthly or as they can to *Immortal Marilyn*. It is constantly growing with new information every month. At the time of its closing, the Immortal Marilyn Fan Club had well over 2,300 members worldwide.

What are some of the highlights of your experiences with Marilyn Monroe fandom?
Meeting people who shared the same love and admiration for Marilyn Monroe was so great. I finally had people to chat with about her life, discussing every aspect of it, and became friends with them. Then becoming President of *Immortal Marilyn* was an incredible experience for me. Taking the fan club from a few hundred fans and nurturing it to become one of the largest and most recognized names in the Marilyn fandom community has been very satisfying, and has made me very proud. *Immortal Marilyn* planned and hosted several fan gatherings in Los Angeles to remember and celebrate the life of Marilyn Monroe. In 2005, we made the homage to New York City to explore all the places Marilyn lived and loved there as well.

Flowers for Marilyn became a very important part of the identity of *Immortal Marilyn*. With contributions of very generous fans, four times a year – Valentine's Day, June 1st for her birthday, August 5th for the Memo-

Fan Appreciation no.1
Mary Sims, Owner of the Immortal Marilyn Fan Club Website

Fig. 2: Flower arrangements from Immortal Marilyn and a memorial card signed by its members for the 52nd anniversary of Marilyn Monroe's passing, August 5, 2014, placed at Marilyn Monroe's crypt, Pierce Bros Westwood Village Memorial Park, Los Angeles. Along with placing cards and flower arrangements on four significant dates each year—Christmas, Valentine's Day, Marilyn's birthday (June 1), and the day of her passing (August 5)—any money leftover from the purchase of the flowers is donated to the charity Animal Haven of New York City, in Marilyn's name and in her honor. For more information, see http:// immortalmarilyn.com/ FlowersForMarilyn.html. (© Jackie Craig)

rial and at Christmas – we place flowers at Marilyn's crypt. The Immortal Marilyn Fan Club has a Los Angeles-based Representative who will go to Marilyn's crypt, clean it and take photos of our flowers to share with the fans online: http://www.immortalmarilyn.com/FlowersForMarilyn.html.

In the early years of *Immortal Marilyn*, over the holidays, the fans would sponsor children at Hollygrove. Long before Marilyn became 'Marilyn' she was a young girl named Norma Jeane. Norma Jeane at one point in her life was taken to live at the Los Angeles Orphanage, which was later renamed 'Hollygrove'. *Immortal Marilyn* would request Christmas wish lists from the children at Hollygrove, and we would match up the children with their own sponsor (an *Immortal Marilyn* member) who would buy the child or children one gift (and sometimes more) from their wish list(s). This tradition continued until Hollygrove moved the children out and into foster homes.

Immortal Marilyn wanted to continue to give in Marilyn's honour. Somewhere around 2006 we decided that Marilyn would surely approve of us setting an amount on what we would spend on flowers for her crypt, and any amount above that would be given to a worthy charity. A poll was taken with several worthy charity choices, and the fans overwhelmingly chose Animal Haven of New York City, a no-kill shelter. This choice was based on Marilyn's love for animals and her adopted city of New York.

Providing a fun place for fans to share their love for and learn more about Marilyn is what *Immortal Marilyn* has always been about.

How would you characterize the Marilyn Monroe fandom communities (a) with which you are involved and (b) as a whole?
Today *Immortal Marilyn*'s fan base is in Facebook. The fans are a mix of the original *Immortal Marilyn* fans from Yahoo! Groups, and the 'newbies', and also a mix of the serious Marilyn fan to the brand new fan.

What are some of the changes/new developments that you have witnessed and/or experienced in Marilyn Monroe fandom communities over the course of your involvement in them?
There are a lot more Marilyn fans with access to each other, which is both

Fig. 3: Immortal Marilyn's
Mary Sims holds a canvas
of a young Marilyn, a recent
addition to her collection
of Marilyn items and
memorabilia. (© Mary Sims)

necessary and great fun. Necessary in being able to learn truths since there is so much misinformation out there about Marilyn. And fun, because fans create great bonds and friendships with each other. That has always been so. Websites have become a lot more sophisticated. Graphic talent of all kinds using Marilyn's image have become quite the thing. The Internet has brought fans together that never would have met otherwise. It has enabled them to meet people who knew Marilyn, photographed her, written books on her, experts from documentaries they'd seen, etc., etc. Been a wonderful thing!

What are some new directions you envision Marilyn Monroe fandom (both yours and the larger fandom community) taking in the future? How do you see yourself involved in them?
I will continue to work on *Immortal Marilyn*'s website with the help of IM's contributors, to give the fans a freshly updated spot every month to come to for Marilyn news and information. I am sure as the Internet becomes more and more sophisticated and evolved, Marilyn's fan base will continue to grow with it.

Are you involved with any other fandom communities? If so, please discuss how these other fandom communities differ from/compare to Marilyn Monroe fandom.
I belong to *Marilyn Remembered*, which is based in Los Angeles, and work with them in making plans for the Memorial. I belong to several other fan-based clubs online, and on Facebook. Each page or group has its own distinct feel. Some in Facebook are more general fan pages while others concentrate on particular aspects of Marilyn, some on collecting memorabilia, some on Marilyn graphics, some on her death for instance. *Immortal Marilyn* has numerous Facebook pages.

What does fandom mean to you/how has fandom impacted your life? What does it mean to you to be part of a fandom community?
Well, it has really changed my life.

Fan Appreciation no.1
Mary Sims, Owner of the Immortal Marilyn Fan Club Website

I became involved with the Marilyn community at a time in my life that was hard. My parents had both recently died, and I found going to the fan clubs online gave me an escape from the sadness and grief for a bit. In time I grew more involved, and was able to put my organizational skills to work for *Immortal Marilyn* and help make it a great place for fans to gather and get their 'Marilyn Fix'. The friends I have met and made via the fandoms online and what they have come to mean to me cannot be measured, truly.

What do you think is Marilyn Monroe's ultimate legacy for her fans?
That anyone can do anything they set their mind on. Norma Jeane was the little girl from nowhere, literally. She claimed in her starlet years that she was dreaming harder than any of the others, and I believe she was right. Marilyn believed in the power of attraction and positive thinking despite her bouts of depression and a background filled with insecurity. She placed positive affirmations on her bathroom mirror and told herself she was worthy. Marilyn was also a true advocate of the underdog, perhaps because she grew up an underdog herself. She was very complex, prone to sadness and depression, but with an iron will to succeed and thrive. She was kind and humble and not interested in material possessions. She never gave up, and she became one of the most incredible legends of the silver screen the world has ever known. She is truly immortal, we only need say her first name, Marilyn... and everyone knows. There is only one Marilyn. Never before, never again.

Please feel free to add more about your involvement in Marilyn Monroe fandom.
It has been my honour to be acknowledged in several publications for my contributions to Marilyn's legacy [Editor's note: including Michelle Morgan's *Marilyn Monroe: Private and Undisclosed*.] I am proud of *Immortal Marilyn*'s place in the Marilyn community and how we strive to share the truth about Marilyn and her life. I hope I will be in a position for the rest of my life to be able to do that for Marilyn. She deserves so much better than what she often gets. Still she is like cream, rises to the top no matter what. God rest her precious soul. ●

(Interview has been edited and condensed)

Biographical note:
Mary Sims was born and raised in Wabasha, Minnesota (home of the film *Grumpy Old Men* [Donald Petrie, 1993, Warner Bros./John Davis Productions]), and is 55 years old. She has been married to the love of her life for 33 years, and they have lived in Austin, Minnesota for 29 years. She has a son, a daughter, a stepson and five beautiful grandchildren. She has been blessed to be able to be a stay-at-home mom. She loves working on her *Immortal Marilyn* website in her spare time. Several times a month it is updated, and every month it gets a whole new look, photo section, monthly book review, etc. She also loves reading, crafts, party planning and spending time with family and friends.

~~~~~~~~~~

GO FURTHER

Books
Marilyn Monroe: Private and Undisclosed
Michelle Morgan
(London: Constable & Robinson, 2012; rev. exp. edn)

Goddess: The Secret Lives of Marilyn Monroe
Anthony Summers
(New York: Macmillan, 1985)

Online
Articles
'Mary Sims – One of Marilyn Monroe's Biggest Fans'
Amanda A. Brooks
Yahoo! Voices. 30 August 2013, http://voices.yahoo.com/mary-sims-one-marilyn-monroes-biggest-fans-12295145.html?cat=40.

'The Days of Her Life: A Most Complete Timeline of Marilyn's Days'
Mary Sims
Immortal Marilyn (n.d.), http://www.immortalmarilyn.com/Timeline.html.

Websites
Immortal Marilyn: http://www.immortalmarilyn.com
Flowers for Marilyn: http://www.immortalmarilyn.com/FlowersForMarilyn.html

Fan Appreciation no.1
Mary Sims, Owner of the Immortal Marilyn Fan Club Website

Marilyn Remembered: http://marilynremembered.org/?hg=0
Animal Haven: http://www.animalhavenshelter.org/
Hollygrove's Norma Jean Gala, March 18, 2014, with Master of
Ceremonies Busy Phillips: http://hollygrove.org/gala/

Social media
Mary Sims's Twitter: @ZeldaZonk
Immortal Marilyn's Facebook pages (closed groups) include Immortal
Marilyn, Immortal Marilyn 2017 Marilyn Monroe Memorial Plans, and
Immortal Marilyn's Death Deliberation Roundtable
Immortal Marilyn Quote UnQuote: https://www.facebook.com/
ImmortalMarilynQuoteUnQuote

Facebook fan groups (Selection)
Marilyn Always and Forever
Marilyn Monroe: The Life and the Legend
Marilyn Remembered Fan Club
Marilyn Monroe Buying and Selling Forum
Marilyn Monroe The Exclusive Tribute Group
Marilyn Our Angel
The Official Marilyn Monroe Fan Club

MARILYN 'WAS A STYLE VISIONARY WHOSE FASHION-FORWARD CHOICES HAVE TRANSCENDED ANY SPECIFIC ERA.

CHRISTOPHER NICKENS AND GEORGE ZENO, AUTHORS
MARILYN IN FASHION: THE ENDURING INFLUENCE OF MARILYN MONROE

Chapter
2

Lipstick Thespians: Being Marilyn Monroe after 5 August 1962

Ross Sloan

→ Let's start with a truism: the work of many celebrity impersonators is akin to the work of gravediggers. To be someone else - who is, of course, someone else's dearly departed - requires that you exhume a body and reanimate a corpse. There is a famous scene with gravediggers in Shakespeare's *Hamlet* (c.1599-1602). The most famous Shakespearean actor of Marilyn Monroe's generation, Laurence Olivier, called that actress 'beautifully dumb', 'a professional amateur' and a 'bitch'. But we will get back to the bard's gravediggers and the glamorous blonde.

So let's start again with a true story: in 2002, the eminent physicist Stephen Hawking celebrated his 60th birthday, a milestone for a man who for decades had persevered and published widely despite being afflicted by a motor neuron disease. Here is how the festivities began, as described in the *New York Times*:

there was emotion tonight in the high-ceilinged hall of Gonville and Caius College here when a butler opened a door and a Marilyn Monroe impersonator slithered in, wearing a pink dress and singing 'I Wanna Be Loved by You' in a whispery voice to Dr. Stephen Hawking, the Cambridge University cosmologist and best-selling author. Dr. Hawking was lolling in a wheelchair, his face split by a huge grin, while some 200 hard-core physicists, their families and friends roared and cheered.

There is a certain dissonance about this, yes? The man of genius pleased by an actress whose work is most often dismissed as cheap entertainment. The man who has cheated death serenaded by the silken ghost of the dead starlet. It may be that believing the fictive dream is as close as we will ever get to the time travel that astrophysicists like Stephen Hawing recognize as theoretically possible and technologically impossible, and it may be that everyone gets what they want for their birthdays. In a 2010 article for the *Daily Mail*, Stephen Hawking wrote, 'I'm obsessed by time. If I had a time machine I'd visit Marilyn Monroe in her prime or drop in on Galileo as he turned his telescope to the heavens.' The universe gives us the brilliant Englishman wanting to visit the enticing American he jokingly calls 'an old girlfriend of mine'. She comes to him, to us, not through a wormhole, but up from a hole in the ground. [Editor's note: In the Stephen Hawking biopic *The Theory of Everything* (James Marsh, 2014), professional Marilyn Monroe impersonator Suzie Kennedy appears, as Marilyn, in a still photograph].

To return to the scene in *Hamlet* with the gravediggers: the enigmatic Prince Hamlet comes upon two clownish men who, spades in hand, are preparing the final resting place for Ophelia, the young noblewoman who had very surely gone mad and very likely drowned herself. The problem with digging fresh graves in old Danish churchyards is that you never know who will turn up. Their spades quickly unearth some bones and a few fleshless skulls. Prince Hamlet, a deep thinker, pauses to recognize and philosophize about how death makes distinct persons into such anonymous artefacts. When one of the skulls is revealed to be that of Yorick, Hamlet, who remembers that court jester for pleasing him well and playing with him as a child, takes the skull in hand and delivers a monologue about existential horror:

Here hung those lips that I have kissed I know
not how oft. Where be your gibes now? your
gambols? your songs? your flashes of merriment,
that were wont to set the table on a roar? (Act V, scene 1)

Lipstick Thespians: Being Marilyn Monroe after 5 August 1962
Ross Sloan

Hamlet, as a nostalgic fan of this now-gone performer, asks questions that have no sure answer. Where do we go when we die? What is the 'us' that survives to go somewhere? Do the jokes outlive the jester? The answers will not be found in Shakespeare or *The Seven Year Itch* (Billy Wilder, 1955). What is sure, though, is that an age of media makes something like immortality for performers all the more possible, a condition that makes the celebrity impersonator's theatricality all that much easier for fans to accept and expect. We have more than Marilyn Monroe's skull today. We have her face.

Marilyn Monroe lives on in images and moving images that are copied again and again, watched again and again, and the more iconic they become the more she, too, seems to have cheated death. The epics of the ancient world were interested in the durability of a name, but the modern world – a world where epic has a new and popularized meaning – allows for the durability of name *and* of face, of voice, of wink, of white dress tossed in an updraft. Think of any poster of Marilyn Monroe, the possibilities of eye-to-eye contact with a woman who died decades ago. Oliver Wendell Holmes, the nineteenth-century writer and jurist, realized just how thoroughly photography had revolutionized the insistent problem of mortality:

> those whom we love no longer leave us in dying, as they did of old. They remain with us just as they appeared in life; they look down upon us from our walls; they lie upon our tables; they rest upon our bosoms.

This may seem a rather aggrandized statement if one remembers that realistic portraits had been commissioned by patrons since, well, at least the Roman funeral portraits from the early centuries of the Common Era's first millennium. But viewers read painting as the work of an artist, a collection of masterful brushstrokes rendering a realistic vision of life, whereas those who view photographs tend to forget the technician (also, of course, an artist) behind the camera. Photographs are not thought of as being like reality. They are reality. George Barris's photographs of Marilyn on Santa Monica Beach in the summer of 1962 are more forcefully haunted than anything that Sandro Botticelli or Lucian Freud could put to canvas. These are the type of photographic images – and perhaps most prominent of these should be Richard Avedon's 1957 portrait of Marilyn – that make the irrational fear that photography can steal the soul start to make sense.

Richard Avedon recalled that studio session with a wine-drunk Marilyn many years later:

> For hours she danced and sang and flirted and did this thing that's – she did Marilyn Monroe. Then there was the inevitable drop [...] she sat in the corner like a child, with everything gone [...] I wouldn't photograph her without her knowledge of it. And as I came with the camera, I saw that she was not saying no.

That portrait, perhaps one of the most famous in the history of photography, was the last frame that Avedon shot that day. What he had witnessed was what makes Marilyn Monroe so attractive to impersonate: she, too, was a Marilyn Monroe impersonator. Her blousy flirtatiousness, her body confidence, her all-consuming *blondeness*, these were all – if the Richard Avedons are to be believed – naught more than a whole life made into a daily performing art piece. The Irish novelist John Banville's 'sleepless nights' were brought on by a boyhood trip to the movie theatre and seeing Marilyn as a 'gorgeously dripping naiad' in *River of No Return* (Otto Preminger, 1954). In eulogizing her, Banville seconds Richard Avedon's interpretation:

> What made MM so bewitching was the very fact that she was – that it was – all or almost all an act. There is the famous story of her walking with a friend down Fifth Avenue in a headscarf and raincoat, as ordinary as anyone else on the street, discussing fame and celebrity and what it was to be a star. 'Do you want me to be her?' Marilyn said to the friend. 'Watch.' And taking off the headscarf and opening her coat to thrust out her chest, she went into the MM sashay, and within half a minute was surrounded by a baying mob of fans and autograph hunters. If the story is true, it gives the lie to the contention that it took five hours of preparation every time for her to 'become' Marilyn.

In his book *A Short History of Celebrity* (2010), Fred Inglis pauses to pay particular attention to Marilyn, the woman that he declares 'was at the center of the national imagination and kept there by a million flashbulbs in a way that no other woman had been or would be in American history'. Out of the steady glare of the spotlight and the staccato light of flashbulbs steps the modern Marilyn Monroe impersonator. More than fifty years after her death there is still a market for Marilyn.

Erika Smith, a Marilyn Monroe impersonator based in Manhattan, can make thousands of dollars a day for her imitative art. She does corporate events and birthdays, the occasional commercial, and in 2012 was flown to perform at a wedding in Beirut and in front of a crowd of thousands in Egypt. A woman named Zahava, who defines herself as 'Canada's top Marilyn Monroe Impersonator', can be booked for parties, corporate functions, singing telegrams, weddings, birthdays, anniversaries, conventions and trade shows. Jami Deadly, based out of Dallas, has acted the part of the actress/singer/model in venues as dissimilar as luxurious Las Vegas casinos and the Texas State Fair or Dallas Arboretum. There is no doubt that some of these impersonators, at least the best of them, are capable of entertaining ardent Marilyn Monroe fans as well as those who know her only for her curves and breathy, baby-girl voice. Maybe the best of them, like the original, leave audiences wanting more. But what do they really want?

It may be that Arthur Miller, married to the real thing for nearly five years (1956–61),

Lipstick Thespians: Being Marilyn Monroe after 5 August 1962
Ross Sloan

offers a hint to Marilyn's life after death in the character of Maggie from his play *After the Fall* (1964). That this Maggie was a version of the woman who had been his Marilyn was not lost on audiences. Some were even unsettled to watch Maggie – needy, self-destructive and suicidal – swallowing handfuls of pills onstage less than seventeen months after news of the demise of Marilyn Monroe made its way around the world. At the end of Act II, which is also the end of her life, Maggie asks Quentin – a celebrated Jewish intellectual just like Arthur Miller – 'Quentin, what's Lazarus?' Her husband's response is that, 'Jesus raised him from the dead. In the Bible. Go to sleep now.' Maggie misses the pronoun and, treating Lazarus as a woman, replies that 'Jesus must have loved her'. Quentin picks up on this and enthusiastically declares, 'That's right, yes! He … loved her enough to raise her from the dead.' So what do they really want? What do the fans, whose love outlasts physical death, want from these performers who make their living making them believe? They want more than verisimilitude. They want something wholly convincing. They want a holy miracle. They want resurrection.

Some of the best evidence for this claim comes from testimonials taken from the website for Jami Deadly:

> 'Good talent is hard to find, but this girl has got it! Every word, spoke or sung, every pose is perfect… she's got to be Marilyn reincarnated!'
> 'Oh Jami, you were so fantastic at my granddaughter's 13th birthday party! She was sooo surprised, and thought Marilyn had risen from the grave!'

The website for Marilyn Monroe impersonator Sheri Winkelmann offers similar testimonials, ones that erase the half century of Marilyn's absence and negate her death. One satisfied customer attributes Sheri as being capable of a 'complete transformation', and another reports on her transcendence: 'She became Marilyn Monroe in every sense, every way. There was not a single person in the audience who didn't believe that somehow, some way, the real Marilyn Monroe was standing, talking, singing and acting right there on stage in front of us.' The concept of celebrity impersonators as more than they are, as more than actors or actresses who have concentrated and capitalized on the role of a lifetime, the role of someone else's life, is alive and well amongst audiences. So how do these celebrity impersonators refine their performances? They do as the fans do, which is to watch Marilyn Monroe movies. They can get the clothes and make-up just right, pick up on the mannerisms, and learn to look like, talk like, move like and be like any Marilyn in any of her feature films. You can do it if you are a professional entertainer in gaudy Atlantic City or if you are a housewife in suburban Illinois. All Marilyn Monroe movies function as instructional videos for how to be a Marilyn Monroe impersonator.

The fact that Marilyn Monroe often played similar characters probably makes the task of the impersonator that much easier. Late in Marilyn's career, typecast too many times and derided by serious and self-important actors, she tried to be something

Fig. 1: Michelle Williams as Marilyn Monroe and Sir Kenneth Branagh as Sir Laurence Olivier during the making of Olivier's The Prince and the Showgirl (1957) in Simon Curtis' 2011 film My Week with Marilyn (© The Weinstein Company).

more than frivolous and sexy. She hired Lee Strasberg as an acting coach and couched dreams of being in Anton Chekov and Henrik Ibsen plays. She earned some grudging respect for her acting abilities with *The Prince and the Showgirl* (Laurence Olivier, 1957), one of her last films. Without seeing the film, can you guess who played the showgirl? Whatever maturation of craft she demonstrated over her thirteen-year acting career was not enough to overcome the roles that seem to be written for her, the kinds of roles that it would now be hard for any actress to play without reminding audiences of Marilyn Monroe. These limitations, which is to say these limited roles, probably contributed more to growing her as a legend and icon than almost anything else she did or could have done. That she was static only made her seem more eternal. That she seems eternal, a result of the on-camera roles chosen for her and the role she chose to play in front of any and every camera, is what makes her available to an imitative art. One does not act as Marilyn. One becomes Marilyn because, really, Marilyn herself was always in character and only had the one character. Richard Avedon remarked that, 'there was no such person as Marilyn Monroe [...] she was invented, like an author creates a character'. Hers has been an act easy to follow and, for some, easy to master and make money off of. She is so unmistakable. She is only... her. Can you imagine a struggling actress trying to earn bookings and extra money, with Meryl Streep impersonations? Which Meryl Streep would she impersonate?

So maybe on 21 June 1983 the *National Examiner* had it just about right with their bold headline reading 'Marilyn Monroe is Alive!' Even if we may doubt the details, and in this case the argument was that she had been confined in a state insane asylum for 22 years after the government faked her death, the mere existence and the proliferation of Marilyn Monroe impersonators proves the truth of that sensational and sensationalistic headline. The version of herself that Marilyn Monroe was able to act was a version that made people happy. Now, money can't buy happiness, and almost everyone acknowledges as much, but that doesn't stop people from spending and spending in pursuit of it. Like Stephen Hawking and what he would do with his hypothetical time machine, those who are most invested in Marilyn are those who want more than a simulacrum, more than some ditzy doppelgänger, they want her, body and soul. One professional impersonator interviewed by sociology professor Kerry O. Ferris tries to give the people what they want:

when I get ready to do Marilyn, I start meditating. I believe in Jesus, you know, and that people have spirits and souls, and that we can communicate with those spirits, even though we're not supposed to, you know? So I really felt Marilyn come into me then, and I said 'Alright, Marilyn baby, let's do it! Here we go,' and I was so great that night.

We want to believe in greatness. We want to share in it. We want to believe that the fame and some flicker of essence outlast the flesh. So the Marilyn Monroe impersona-

Lipstick Thespians: Being Marilyn Monroe after 5 August 1962
Ross Sloan

tor invites the possibility of being even a momentary mani-
festation of the totality of the woman that was. We'll buy
that. We'll pay for that. We want to believe in immortality,
even if not for ourselves.

As Hamlet asks the gravedigger about the hole he has
dug, 'Who is to be buried in it?' The gravedigger's reply is
'One that was a woman, sir; but, rest her soul, she's dead.'
Hamlet complains that the gravedigger is being 'absolute',
and he is. The preservation of celebrity images, the celebrity afterlife in still or moving images, subverts what once
was accepted to be the absoluteness of death. The celebrity impersonator is a living
person who takes the stage to offer something like a second life for the celebrity. The
ancients built monuments to the famous dead. We don't like quarried limestone blocks
or the inorganic coldness of marble. We like our monuments to be living monuments.
Marilyn Monroe is in a brass coffin in a crypt at Corridor of Memories #24, at the Westwood Village Memorial Park Cemetery in Los Angeles. And she isn't. The gravedigger in
Hamlet boasts that 'the houses he makes last 'til doomsday'. But they don't. The dead
get up, get out, play dress up, paint faces at thirteenth birthday parties, sing to physicists, and earn rave reviews from beyond the grave. The famous that we think we own
– the moment that Norma Jeane Baker became Marilyn Monroe was the same moment
she became *our* Marilyn Monroe – cannot rest in peace. Our restlessness about the mu-
tability associated with time and our hesitant acceptance of even our own mortality
would never allow for that. Neither can the market forces. It is supply and demand. She
is dead, and so a boutique industry of impersonators who now keep pink satin gowns and
fake diamond chokers in their closets springs to life. She died, and we weren't done with
her. The show – and the showgirl – must go on.

What we know of the Marilyn Monroe that was tells us that she probably wouldn't
mind that her likeness has long outlived her. A friend of hers told a story of seeing her
staring into a mirror, totally self-absorbed, and to return again much later to still find
her staring into that same mirror. This friend asked her to explain herself. Then Marilyn
Monroe said of the reflected image of Marilyn Monroe that, 'I'm looking at her.' This is
categorically different than saying 'I'm looking at myself.' The image became more real
than the self and this takeover, whether intentional or unbidden, gives us the Marilyn
that can go on and on. In her time all the world was her stage, and in our time all the
world is a mirror, or a hall of mirrors, reflection upon reflection upon reflection. Maggie
didn't know who or what Lazarus was. She thought he was a she and, we see, she was
right. Marilyn is Lazarus. She can unzip the LA County body bag, open the crypt, roll
back the stone, and she is once more among the quick with nothing more required than
a blonde wig, a false mole, the singing voice like a child's whispered prayer, and that
white dress that dances on air and through the currents of time. ●

*Fig. 2: The Memorial Card
for Marilyn Monroe, signed
by members of Immortal
Marilyn, placed at Marilyn's
crypt along with the flower
arrangements donated by
the fan club to commemorate
the 52nd anniversary of her
death, August 5, 2014. (©
Jackie Craig)*

*Fig. 3: World renowned
professional Marilyn Monroe
lookalike Suzie Kennedy
at Marilyn Monroe's crypt
(©Suzie Kennedy).*

GO FURTHER

Books
'Sun-Painting and Sun-Sculpture: With a Stereoscopic Trip Across the Atlantic' in
Soundings from the Atlantic
Oliver Wendell Holmes
(Boston: Ticknor and Fields, 1864)

Marilyns Are a Guy's Best Friend
Joseph L. Clough and Tessa Winston
(Coffeetable Press, 2011)

A Short History of Celebrity
Fred Inglis
(Princeton: PUP, 2010)

Richard Avedon Portraits
Essays by Maria Morris Hambourg, Mia Fineman and Richard Avedon; Foreword by
Philippe de Montebello
(New York: Harry N. Abrams/Metropolitan Museum of Art, 2002)

Plays
After the Fall
Arthur Miller
(New York: Viking Press, 1964)

The Tragedy of Hamlet, Prince of Denmark
William Shakespeare (c.1599–1602)
(Folger Shakespeare Library edition, Simon and Schuster, 2003)

Extracts/Essays/Articles
'Building Characters: The Work of Celebrity Impersonators'
Kerry O. Ferris
In *The Journal of Popular Culture.* 44: 6 (2011): 1191-1208.

Online
Articles
'After Marilyn, Jimmy James Finds his Own Voice (Plus Some More)'

Lipstick Thespians: Being Marilyn Monroe after 5 August 1962
Ross Sloan

BeBe Sweetbriar
EDGE on the Net. 22 May 2014, http://www.edgeonthenet.com/entertainment/the-atre/reviews//159360/after_marilyn,_jimmy_james_finds_his_own_voice_%28plus_some_more%29.

'John Banville on Marilyn Monroe 50 Years after Her Death'
John Banville
The Guardian. 3 August 2012, http://www.theguardian.com/books/2012/aug/03/marilyn-monroe-banville-50-death.

'How to Build a Time Machine'
Stephen Hawking
Daily Mail. 27 April 2010, http://www.dailymail.co.uk/home/moslive/article-1269288/STEPHEN-HAWKING-How-build-time-machine.html.

'A Marvel of Science, Hawking Turns 60'
Dennis Overbye
The New York Times. 9 January 2002, http://www.nytimes.com/2002/01/09/world/a-marvel-of-science-hawking-turns-60.html.

Marilyn Monroe tribute/lookalike artists' websites
Jami Deadly, Award Winning Marilyn Monroe Tribute Artist/Impersonator/Lookalike/Jami as MM: http://www.modernmarilyn.com
The Marilyn Monroe Tribute Show, Featuring Zahava: http://www.marilynmonroeshow.com
Erika Smith as Marilyn Monroe, Marilyn Monroe Impersonator and Tribute Artist: http://marilynmonroetributeartist.com
Sheri Winkelmann, Marilyn Monroe Impersonator, Singer and Actress: http://marilyn-shows.com
Memory Monroe (Dutch-born Singer and Actress Claudia Kooj): http://www.memory-monroe.com/home
Holly Beavon, Marilyn Monroe Lookalike-Impersonator: http://www.hollybeavon.com/marilyn-monroe-look-alike.html
Jimmy James: The Marilyn Years: http://www.youtube.com/playlist?list=PL3C26FD1E5C941687

Works of Art
Richard Avedon, *Marilyn Monroe, actress, New York* (1957). Gelatin silver print, printed 1989, 7 15/16in. × 7 13/16in. (20.2cm × 19.8cm). Museum of Modern Art (MoMA) Learn-ing, http://www.moma.org/learn/moma_learning/richard-avedon-marilyn-monroe-actress-new-york-may-6-1957.

Fig. 1: Debra Monroe as
Marilyn Monroe (courtesy
Deborah Bakker).

Interviews with and statements from Marilyn Monroe lookalike artists Deborah Bakker ('Debra Monroe'), Susan Griffiths and Suzie Kennedy:

Deborah Bakker, aka 'Debra Monroe', Marilyn Monroe/ Norma Jeane Lookalike Artist
Questions by Marcelline Block

How did you become a Marilyn Monroe fan?

My uncle is a fan of hers. When I was 16 – almost 17 years old – he said that someday I would look like Marilyn Monroe, and I replied, 'who is she?' So he showed me his clock with a picture of Marilyn on it, and later, he also showed me some pictures of her when she was Norma Jeane, before she became Marilyn Monroe. I was curious about who she was, so I googled her, and read about her childhood experiences. I closely identified with her. And because my uncle said I looked like her, I gained more confidence in myself, since I'm somewhat self-conscious about my own appearance. Then I started a Facebook account in 2011, and saw that there are many Marilyn fan groups, so I became a member of some of those groups. I then met people who are also big fans of Marilyn Monroe and they helped me to learn a lot more about her. She is a true icon for many people, and she deserves to be honoured.

Why do you want to be a Marilyn Monroe lookalike?

I love to be a lookalike primarily as Norma Jeane Baker because most people don't know about this time in Marilyn Monroe's life. And it's a pity because, when she was Norma Jeane, she was very natural and more herself than when she became Marilyn. She was also discovered at the time when she was Norma Jeane. That's why I want to show this period in her life. I also do the blonde Marilyn, and the reason why I want to do this is because it gives me a happy feeling, and I want to keep her spirit alive.

Where have you performed as Norma Jeane and Marilyn?

I have performed on June 1, 2012 at a festival in Holland for art and music called Het Holland Festival. I also performed at a Winter Fair, on December 6, 2013, where they were selling Christmas merchandise and many other winter items. My performances in 2014 included an outdoors 1950s event on June 21, with old-fashioned

Lipstick Thespians: Being Marilyn Monroe after 5 August 1962
Ross Sloan

cars and many vintage clothes and items that people can buy; a summer fair on June 29; an event called 'Feel the 1950s', on August 31, also in Holland (in Venlo), where people performed in '50s bands as well; and a big 'old-timey' fair: All-American Days at Rosmalen Autotron, October 25–26, 2014. Many muscle cars and Hotrods were displayed and people coul buy jukeboxes and vintage clothes, among other things.

(Interview has been condensed and edited)

Biographical note
Deborah Bakker was born on 8 March 1991 in Zaandam, Holland, where she resides. Under the name 'Debra Monroe', she performs as Marilyn Monroe/Norma Jeane.

GO FURTHER

Online
Articles
'Marilyn Monroe's Lost Scrapbook.' *Newsweek*, Special Issue. January 2014, http://www.newsweek.com/newsweek-special-issue-marilyn-monroes-lost-scrapbook-225496.

Websites
Debra Monroe, Lookalike as Marilyn Monroe and Young Marilyn: http://debra-monroe.jouwweb.nl/

Fig. 2: Headshot of Suzie
Kennedy as Marilyn Monroe
(courtesy Suzie Kennedy).

Suzie Kennedy, Marilyn Monroe Lookalike/Tribute Artist
Recounted to Marcelline Block

How It All Began: It all started when people on the street began saying that I looked like Marilyn Monroe. I knew who Marilyn was, but I never saw the resemblance nor even knew what a lookalike/tribute artist did. It was only after meeting a few lookalikes at public places that they too said I looked like Marilyn Monroe. It was getting to the point where it was happening on a daily basis, with people asking me for my picture.

The First Time Playing Marilyn: I was still in college when I was approached to go to a casting for a TV commercial [Editor's note: for After Eight Mints] to play Marilyn. I had no idea what this would entail, but off I went to the audition. I had no Marilyn costumes. However, when I arrived, the casting director rushed over to me, asking me who I was. I saw other 'Marilyns' sitting there, all in character with books and dresses, and there I was, wearing just my black spaghetti strap dress. I auditioned and it seemed to just come from within me when I was asked to do Marilyn's voice and the mannerisms. I got the part, and a few days later I was on set at the film studios with supermodel Naomi Campbell, and I was playing Marilyn Monroe. They had a made to measure dress for me, the first evening gown I had ever owned, let alone had been made for me. It was a replica of what Marilyn had worn in *Gentleman Prefer Blondes* [Howard Hawks, 1953]. Jobs continued to come in for me. It's a funny business in that if you do really good jobs the feedback and the word gets around, and before you know it you are suddenly working very regularly.

In Marilyn's Clothes: One of my most amazing gigs was when I was asked to model Marilyn Monroe's actual clothing from her personal life and her movies. I will never forget the moment when I put on the red sequined dress from *Gentleman Prefer Blondes*. It fit me perfectly, and I thought how bizarre it was that my first image of Marilyn was her in this actual dress at the beginning of the film and here I am, standing in that dress over fifty years later! It was really amazing and an experience I will never forget. I also wore that dress on live TV. My other favourite outfit to wear was her original costume from *Some Like It Hot* [Billy Wilder, 1959]. The film is probably her most famous and to wear the actual dress was incredible. I feel like I could not get any closer to the original than to be in her actual clothing. There's something very personal about that. I also modelled for the auction houses like Christie's when their Marilyn items came up. Luckily, I was able to buy some of her personal property myself: I own her two awards from the big Christie's sale of her personal possessions. I also own her bank book and a service card from her funeral. It is really sad to hold that.

Playing Marilyn On-screen: One of the most amazing experiences is to play Marilyn

Lipstick Thespians: Being Marilyn Monroe after 5 August 1962
Ross Sloan

on film, and I have done this a few times. I have played her in reconstruction documentaries, usually about how she died. People are still fascinated by the mystery of it. I also had to play her in the Kennedy biography, *JFK: Seven Days That Made a President* [Steve Webb, 2013], singing 'Happy Birthday, Mr. President'. To play these roles you have mixed emotions. You really start to get into the mindset of how Marilyn felt when you are in studios made to look like her own home [and] also having to read scripts of words that she said. I made a feature film in Italy, *Io & Marilyn* [2009], with the famous Italian director/actor Leonardo Pieraccioni. This was an amazing film as it was starring a very well-known actor in Italy and the film made number one at the box office. I was the co-star, playing the ghost of Marilyn Monroe, and the estate had to give permission for my look – which they did. I was on billboards all over Italy, on TV shows, in magazines such as *Vanity Fair* and other publications/newspapers. It was also lovely as they made Marilyn's character sweet and kind, the Marilyn I'd imagine her to be. The Italians have much affection for Marilyn.

Singing Marilyn's Songs: I also have my own one woman show as Marilyn. I perform all over the world, but I recently have had a sold-out show in Helsinki, Finland. I love to sing the famous Marilyn songs, my favourite being 'I Wanna Be Loved by You' [Herbert Stothart and Bert Kalmar, 1928]. That song is just so Marilyn to me. And everybody knows it. I also incorporate other songs that Marilyn didn't sing but that her idols, like Ella Fitzgerald, sang. Ella has songs that suit Marilyn's tone and you can see why Marilyn studied Ella as she has really helped me also get the Marilyn tone to my voice when I sing.

Getting into the Marilyn Mindset: When I have the costume, the hair and the make-up on and am about to do a gig, my whole mindset is in Marilyn mode. It is acting. But as I only ever act one character, I have learned to master my craft. I know what works and how to react with an audience. You have to make them feel like they really are meeting Marilyn. It sounds crazy as they know you are not her, but everyone wants to play the game for a moment as it's fun.

Honouring Marilyn's Memory: I take the responsibility of my job seriously, and never do jobs I feel will disrespect or hurt her memory. She has given me a great life and livelihood through looking like her. I've travelled the world and made great friends, all because of this lady. I feel a unique closeness and protectiveness of her due to what she has given me. She is like a long lost relative I never met but feel I know. Marilyn and I have had similar things happen in life to us growing up and also just trying to be a glamorous girl in what can be a hard world. She always tried and so do I. I feel very lucky for the experiences I have had playing her and I know one day it will come to an end as age beats us all, but it has been the best job ever and I have Marilyn to thank for that. She's an icon and her fame is not diminishing. It's getting bigger. I am travelling more and new generations write to me about her. I guess they feel sometimes that I'm the next best thing as they can't talk with her. I try my best to keep her memory alive and I feel blessed I have had these opportunities that most fans of Marilyn would have done for free and I've been paid to do. I would say to any girl wanting to impersonate Marilyn that they should do it. If they study her and go into it with a pure heart and love of the artist they portray they will have a great time. And also hold onto the fact that you are not Marilyn. You are simply bringing her back for entertainment for people. It's easy to believe your own publicity when you get so much attention but there will only ever be the real Marilyn and she will continue long after I have retired and passed on and no one remembers my name.

Visiting Marilyn's Grave: When I visited her grave for the first time, it was such a strange experience because it finally felt real. She was a real person, not just this movie star; she was a real person, and here I was standing at her graveside, she was only 36 and gone. I cannot thank her enough for all the times she has brought me and I only wish she could have found her happiness and still be here so that I could thank her personally.

(Statement has been condensed and edited)

Biographical note
Born in Grants Pass, Oregon (USA), Suzie Kennedy was raised in London. For over fifteen years, she has been a professional Marilyn Monroe lookalike/tribute artist.

GO FURTHER

Online
Websites/Social media
Suzie Kennedy as Marilyn Monroe: www.marilynmonroelookalike.co.uk
Twitter: *@SuzieKennedy*

Films (in which Suzie Kennedy appears as Marilyn Monroe)
JFK: Seven Days That Made a President, Steve Webb, dir. (Great Britain: Blast! Films, 2013).
Io & Marilyn, Leonardo Pieraccioni, dir. (Italy: Medusa Film/Levante Film, 2009).
The Theory of Everything (in a still photograph), James Marsh, dir. (Great Britain: Working Title Films, 2014)

Television
'Who Killed Marilyn Monroe?' Michael Waterhouse, dir., *Revealed* (Great Britain: 3MB Television, 2003).

Songs
'I Wanna Be Loved by You.' Music by Herbert Stothart and Harry Ruby; lyrics by Bert Kalmar (1928). Sung by Marilyn Monroe in *Some Like It Hot* (Billy Wilder, 1959, United States: Ashton Productions/The Mirsch Corporation).

Lipstick Thespians: Being Marilyn Monroe after 5 August 1962
Ross Sloan

Susan Griffiths, Professional Marilyn Monroe Lookalike/Tribute Artist
Recounted to Marcelline Block

I started portraying Marilyn because as a young brunette, people always told me I looked like Marilyn. A photographer named James Mares turned me into Marilyn as I had no idea.

I started in the original cast of *Legends in Concert*, and went on to star in a movie of the week called *Marilyn and Me* for ABC (John Patterson, 1991). Played her in *Quantum Leap*, *Curb Your Enthusiasm*, *Nip/Tuck*. My video played behind Elton John in his 'Candle in the Wind' (1973) segment [Editor's note: in his 'Red Piano Revue' in Las Vegas]. I do corporate events as well, my boyfriend [Editor's note: Andrew DiMino] portrays Dean Martin and we do a crooner and a bombshell show. I just completed the Marilyn Monroe film and theatre cruise [Editor's note: Crystal Cruises], where I performed as Marilyn. I have many amazing stories, Marilyn has been an incredible journey.

Fig. 3: Susan Griffiths as Marilyn Monroe (photo courtesy Susan Griffiths).

Biographical note
Susan Griffiths, called 'the No. 1 Marilyn' by the *Los Angeles Times*'s Gina Piccalo, appears as Marilyn Monroe in many films (*Pulp Fiction* [Quentin Tarantino, 1994]), television shows (*Curb Your Enthusiasm*, *Nip/Tuck*, *Quantum Leap*), theatrical productions, advertisements, and corporate events. As Marilyn Monroe, she graced the cover of *GQ*'s 'Presidential' issue (November 2008) with Jimmy Kimmel posing as JFK. She received the Cloney Award for Most Outstanding Impersonation of a Female Film Legend. She has worked with Rosanna Arquette, Scott Bakula, Zack Braff, Steve Buscemi, Jamie Foxx, Peter Greene, Joel Grey, Dustin Hoffman, Dennis Hopper, Samuel L. Jackson, Harvey Keitel, Hilary Swank, Quentin Tarantino, John Travolta, Christopher Walken and Bruce Willis, among others.

GO FURTHER

Magazines
Interview, 35th Anniversary Issue, October 2004.

Online
Articles
'Crystal Cruises Stages a Tribute to Marilyn Monroe Hollywood Spectacular at Sea'
Patti Pietschmann
Examiner.com. 14 January 2013, http://www.examiner.com/article/crystal-cruises-stages-a-tribute-to-marilyn-monroe-hollywood-spectacular-at-sea.

'We've Got the Stars – and a Lot of the Impersonators'
Gina Piccalo
Los Angeles Times. 5 January 2003, http://articles.latimes.com/2003/jan/05/entertainment/ca-piccalo05.

'On View: The Woman Who Would be Monroe'
Susan King
Los Angeles Times. 22 September 1991, http://articles.latimes.com/1991-09-22/news/tv-3742_1_marilyn-monroes-griffiths.

'*Marilyn & Dean:* A Toast to Dean Martin and Marilyn Monroe.' *CMIEntertainment.com*
(n.d.), http://www.cmientertainment.com/MartinAndMonroe.html.

Websites
Susan Griffiths as Marilyn Monroe: http://www.susangriffiths.com/
Legends in Concert – Live Celebrity Tribute Shows: http://www.legendsinconcert.com

Films
Pulp Fiction, Quentin Tarantino, dir. (United States: Miramax/A Band Apart, 1994).
Legends in Concert, Documentary, Ilana Bar-Din, dir. (1991).

Television
With Her, Laurent Morlet, dir. (France: Laurent Morlet Productions, 2012).
[In which Griffiths and DiMino are interviewed.]

Television show episodes and a made-for-television movie (in which Susan Griffiths plays Marilyn Monroe)
'Joyce and Sharon Monroe', Charles Haid, dir., *Nip/Tuck*, Ryan Murphy, creator, Sea-

Lipstick Thespians: Being Marilyn Monroe after 5 August 1962
Ross Sloan

son 5, Episode 2 (United States: Ryan Murphy Productions/Warner Bros. Television/ Shephard Robin Company, 2007).

'The End', Larry Charles, dir., *Curb Your Enthusiasm*, Larry David, creator, Season 5, Episode 10 (United States: Home Box Office, 2005).

'In Her Dreams', Pamela Fryman, dir., *Cybill*, Chuck Lorre, creator, Season 3, Episode 15 (United States: Carsey-Werner Productions, 1997).

'Goodbye Norma Jean – April 4, 1960', Christopher Hibler, dir., *Quantum Leap*, Donald P. Bellisario, creator, Season 5, Episode 18 (United States: Universal TV, 1993).

Marilyn and Me, John Patterson, dir. (United States: Poochie Productions/Samuels Film Company, 1991).

'Happy Halloween: Part II', John Tracy, dir., *Growing Pains*, Neal Marlens, creator, Season 6, Episode 8 (Warner Bros. Television, 1990).

Song:
Elton John, 'Candle in the Wind,' in Elton John, *Goodbye Yellow Brick Road* (1973, DJM Records)

'FIFTY YEARS ON, WE'RE STILL WATCHING HER MOVIES AND TALKING ABOUT HER. THAT'S NOT A DUMB WOMAN, TRUST ME.'

LAUREN BACALL,
MARILYN MONROE'S CO-STAR IN
HOW TO MARRY A MILLIONAIRE

Chapter
3

Marilyn is a *Smash*: Depicting the Icon in NBC's Musical Drama

Raquel Crisóstomo

→ **Despite the fact that more than five decades have passed since the unexpected death of Norma Jeane Baker, aka Marilyn Monroe (1926-1962), the Blonde Bombshell has never left the collective imagination of contemporary culture.**

To cite just a few of the most recent examples, for the 50th anniversary of her death in 2012, Hollywood remembered the actress with *My Week with Marilyn* (Simon Curtis, 2011), featuring Michelle Williams in the titular role. This film is based on the memoir by Colin Clark, which describes the problems Sir Laurence Olivier encountered when directing Marilyn Monroe during the filming of *The Prince and the Showgirl* (1957). Andrew Dominik's forthcoming film *Blonde*, a Marilyn biopic adapted from the novel of the same name by Joyce Carol Oates (published in 2000) and starring Jessica Chastain, is slated for a 2016 release. Lifetime's 2015 television miniseries *Marilyn*, adapted from *The Secret Life of Marilyn Monroe* by J. Randy Taraborelli, features Kelli Garner in the titular role and co-stars Susan Sarandon as Marilyn's mother Gladys.

As part of the wide range of films and television productions dedicated to the actress set up as a myth of popular culture, several recent televised works depict Marilyn as the centre of the narrative. In 2001, CBS brought out *Blonde* (directed by Joyce Chopra) – without much success – a miniseries that adapted the aforementioned work by Joyce Carol Oates, in which Australian-born actress Poppy Montgomery played Norma Jeane Baker, with Titus Welliver and Patrick Dempsey as some of the men in her life. It was a biopic that mixed real facts with fiction: her childhood years; her first marriage to James Dougherty; meeting photographer Otto Ose; her career with Twentieth Century Fox; and her marriages to baseball player Joe DiMaggio (Welliver) and author/playwright Arthur Miller (Dempsey).

The television series *Mad Men* (Matthew Weiner, creator, AMC, 2007–present) alludes to Marilyn: in the episode entitled 'Maidenform' (Season 2, Episode 6, 31 August 2008) the actress is defined as a champion of sensuality. At the start of 'Six Month Leave' (Season 2, Episode 9, 28 September 2008) the commotion caused by Marilyn's death is portrayed brilliantly through the attitude of the women working at the Sterling Cooper advertising agency. This is particularly well demonstrated by the conversation between Joan Holloway (Christina Hendricks) – who identifies with Roslyn Tabor, the character played by Marilyn in *The Misfits* (John Huston, 1961) – and Roger Sterling (John Slattery):

Joan: She [Marilyn] was so young.
Sterling: Not you, too.
Joan: Yes, I'm just another frivolous secretary.
Sterling: It's a terrible tragedy, but that woman is a stranger. Roosevelt. I hated him, but I felt like I knew him.
Joan: *A lot of people felt like they knew her* [emphasis added]. You should be sensitive to that.
Sterling: (Grabs her arm intimately) Hey… you're not like her. […] Physically a little but don't tell me that makes you sad.
Joan: *It's not a joke. This world destroyed her* [emphasis added].
Sterling: Really? She was a movie star who had everything… and everybody. And she threw it away. But hey… if you want to be sad.
Joan: One day you'll lose *someone who is important to you* [emphasis added]. You'll see. It's very painful.

Marilyn is a *Smash*: Depicting the Icon in NBC's Musical Drama
Raquel Crisóstomo

More recently, in the television miniseries *The Kennedys* (Jon Cassar, History Television, 2011), a joint US-Canada production, Canadian actress Charlotte Sullivan portrayed Marilyn Monroe during her relationship with John Fitzgerald Kennedy in the 1960s, in Episode 7, 'The Countdown to Tragedy' (10 April 2011). There are also plans to broadcast *Finding Marilyn*, a reality show which promises to discover the modern version of the blonde icon, in the near future. Produced by Entertainment One Television (eOne), this reality television programme will bring together twelve contestants to compete to be the next great American icon.

But if there is one recent work of televised fiction that focuses on the persona of Marilyn, and which manages to describe the more human side of the myth surrounding her, it's *Smash* (NBC, 2012-13), produced by Steven Spielberg and created by Theresa Rebeck (Rebeck was the showrunner of the series' first season; for its second season, she was replaced by Josh Safran, previously responsible for the 2007-12 CW series *Gossip Girl*). *Smash* narrates the birth and gestation of a Broadway musical called *Bombshell*, which is based on Marilyn's life as conceived and written by the award-winning team of composer Tom Levitt (Christian Borle) and playwright Julia Houston (Debra Messing). Upon learning of their planned musical project, producer Eileen Rand (Anjelica Huston) decides to join the project, bringing with her the brilliant but egomaniacal British stage director Derek Wills (Jack Davenport), while up-and-coming actresses Karen Cartwright (Katherine McPhee) and Ivy Lynn (Megan Hilty) compete to play the Hollywood icon in *Bombshell*. As production of the musical progresses, the various parties involved struggle with their chaotic lives, alongside all the drama that arises when working on a Broadway show.

The cast of *Smash* includes performers who are already acclaimed in the worlds of music, theatre and film, including Norbert Leo Butz, Brian d'Arcy James, Nick Jonas, Jennifer Hudson and Uma Thurman. The songs in the fictional work are composed by Marc Shaiman (*Hairspray* [2007]), Scott Wittman (*Down with Love* [2003]) and Chris Bacon, the first two of whom have won Tony, Grammy and Emmy Awards. *Smash* lasted for two seasons on NBC; this discussion primarily treats the first season of *Smash*, as it is focused on Marilyn and *Bombshell*, while the second season 'introduced *Hit List*, a separate musical' (*Vulture.com/New York Magazine*).

Smash was strategically scheduled to air following the reality television programme *The Voice* (created by John de Mol, NBC, 2011-present), a musical competition show, so that *Smash*, in which music plays a central role, could benefit from a lead-in from *The Voice*. It is no surprise that Katharine McPhee stars in *Smash*, since she was one of the discoveries of the fifth season (2006) of the singing competition reality television show

Fig. 1: The US television series Smash (NBC, 2012-2013) narrates the birth and gestation of Bombshell, a fictional Broadway musical based on Marilyn Monroe's life. (© Madwoman in the Attic)

Fig. 2 In Smash, Ivy Lynn
(Megan Hilty) and Karen
Cartwright (Katharine
McPhee) compete for the
role of Marilyn in the musical
Bombshell. (© Madwoman in
the Attic)

American Idol (created by Simon Fuller, FOX, 2002-present), as that season's runner-up. American Idol is a reality show similar to The Voice, although Idol predates Voice by nearly ten years. As mentioned above, there are also plans to broadcast, in the near future, the reality show Finding Marilyn (Entertainment One Television [eOne]), whose premise is to 'discover' the contemporary version of the platinum-blonde icon from a pool of twelve competitors.

Smash perfectly captures the cultural myth Marilyn has become and approaches her bifurcated essence through the unfolding of the production of Bombshell, specifically the differing interpretations of Marilyn by the two main actresses, Ivy (Hilty) and Karen (McPhee), in their battle for the role. It is particularly relevant to note that in Smash, the character of Marilyn is not only given a biographical treatment – as in the aforementioned previous televised narratives – but also, the show explores the persona of Marilyn, an analysis of the fears, absences and passions embodied both by the character and the woman. While we previously made reference to the 'Maidenform' episode of Mad Men, which presents Marilyn as a topos, in Smash, the opposite occurs, since Smash shows the humanity behind the Marilyn myth without the need to go further into biographical details, which, precisely because of her iconic status, are already well-known and therefore do not need to be enumerated in this context. Thus for example, in Episode 3 of Season 1 of Smash ('Enter Mr. DiMaggio', 20 February 2012), it is not necessary to explain to the viewer Marilyn's relationship with Joe DiMaggio; rather, he is introduced into the cast naturally since we already know the character by reputation as well as for his relationship with Marilyn.

At the heart of Smash, underneath the changing storylines about the show's characters – almost entirely revolving around their love lives – this fiction has tried to go beyond the usual topics associated with the deceased actress. On many occasions there is reference to the apparent strength that Marilyn possessed in spite of her emotional fragility; her romantic relationships, and the eternal Cinderella aura that surrounded her, which is the premise of Finding Marilyn, according to its creators: 'the one-hour series will be a "real-life Cinderella story" that allows twelve young ladies to compete for a chance to make it big in Hollywood and become the next great American icon' (Ashley Lee, SheKnows.com).

In Smash, we can see four different Marilyns: Ivy Lynn who plays the most sensual Marilyn; Karen Cartwright, who portrays the charismatic and talented Marilyn; the Hollywood star version of Marilyn as incarnated by famous contemporary film actress Rebecca Duvall (Uma Thurman); and finally, the vision of stage director Derek Wills, which combines all these aspects, highlighting, above all, Marilyn's vulnerability. During the first season of Smash, the viewer moves between these different facets of the actress through the persistent question asked by the musical: who will be selected to play Marilyn in Bombshell?

Marilyn is a *Smash*: Depicting the Icon in NBC's Musical Drama
Raquel Crisóstomo

From the start, both Ivy and Karen are shown playing Marilyn throughout the musical numbers in the imagined world of the series, so that the viewer can see the differences between their interpretations in more detail: sensual Ivy displays her voluptuousness and emphasizes her extensive experience on Broadway (although in chorus, rather than starring, roles); Karen, a hardworking beginner with natural magnetism that radiates from her first audition, and in her many musical numbers outside of the preparation and rehearsals for *Bombshell* (which are needed in order for *Smash* to function as a Katharine McPhee vehicle); and Rebecca Duvall who, although lacking Ivy's and Karen's musical talent, is still able to use her great manipulation skills and the power she possesses as a Hollywood diva.

Fig. 3: Karen (Katharine McPhee) as Marilyn Monroe in Bombshell.
(© Madwoman in the Attic)

Karen is endowed with the voice, innate charm and talent – as well as what Ivy really wants the most, which is love. She has the love of her childhood friends (Episode 3, 'Enter Mr. DiMaggio'); her attentive boyfriend Dev (Raza Jaffrey), and her caring, traditional Midwestern parents who, despite not really sharing the aspirations of their daughter, support and love her unconditionally ('Pilot', 6 February 2012). Karen is a character who slowly learns about the temptations and dangers of fame from Rebecca, and along the way, loses her boyfriend Dev due to his infidelity – with none other than Ivy – but through these experiences, she becomes a star. As Derek tells her at the end of the season: 'Whatever happens now, don't ever doubt that you're a star' (Episode 15, 'Bombshell', 14 May 2012).

On the contrary, Ivy only has her friends at her side, and against her wishes, she ends up sharing them with Karen. Ivy's love life involves an on-again, off-again relationship with Derek, through whom she initially got the starring role (so she never finds out if it was due to her talent onstage or because she was dating the director); and later, a one-night stand with Dev, Karen's fiancé, after a chance meeting with him in a bar. Finally, Ivy is also denied maternal love, as her mother, Leigh Conroy (played by Broadway legend Bernadette Peters), is a famed Broadway diva with a long career of her own. Interestingly, in 'The Workshop' (Episode 7, 19 March 2012) Conroy performs her signature song, 'Everything's Coming up Roses' from *Gypsy* (Jule Styne, Stephen Sondheim and Arthur Laurents, 1959), a musical in which Peters, in real life, played the role of Rose in 2003, garnering a Tony Award nomination for Best Leading Actress. On *Smash*, Leigh's relationship with her daughter Ivy is vexed, such as when Leigh tells Ivy, upon seeing Marilyn Monroe on television, 'Look at that magnetism. No wonder you're nervous. I don't know how you're gonna pull any of that off' ('The Workshop'). Ivy also becomes addicted to the steroid prednisone, a medication she is forced to take when she strains her vocal cords, clearly a parallel to Marilyn Monroe's own dependency on drugs such as stimulants and tranquilizers.

In the case of Rebecca Duvall (Uma Thurman), her brief appearance in *Bombshell*

Fig. 4: Ivy Lynn (Megan Hilty)
as Marilyn in the first season
of Smash (© Madwoman in
the Attic)

takes us back to Marilyn the star: in fact, Duvall appears for the first time in Season 1, Episode 11 (out of 15), appropriately entitled 'The Movie Star' (16 April 2012). Her role is that of a diva in all her glory, surrounded by fame and money, with power and ambition, but she is also aware that she does not have the talent nor the years of theatrical and vocal training needed to portray the character of Marilyn onstage. When Karen asks her why she is leaving *Bombshell*, Duvall answers: 'I was scared. I've never been so scared in my life. I'm not going back into the show' (Episode 14, 'Previews', 7 May 2012).

From Episode 10 onward, with five remaining in the first season, Derek starts to have visions of Karen portraying Marilyn, such as when he speaks to her or when she performs Ruby & the Romantics's hit 1963 song 'Our Day Will Come' for him in Episode 11. Although this version of Marilyn combines the different attributes we have covered, she stands out for her innocence, which is emphasized by the fact that when she appears in Derek's hallucinations, she is always dressed in a simple outfit instead of one of the glamorous evening gowns worn by Marilyn during the show. This vulnerability, together with her charm, is the reason why, in the end, Karen is the actress chosen to portray Marilyn in *Bombshell*. In fact, after the final casting decision, Ivy asks Derek why he didn't choose her, and he replies: 'I see her… in my head. She just has something that you don't. I'm sorry' (Episode 15). Apparently Karen's version of Marilyn – more vulnerable, sensitive, charming and human – wins, although in reality the most direct heir to Marilyn's legacy turns out to be Ivy, as demonstrated at the end of the season finale episode, which closes with Ivy contemplating taking a handful of pills. The sensual Marilyn played by Ivy is actually the version most closely identified with the conflicts and traumas of the historical Marilyn: like Marilyn, Ivy also has a more than troubled relationship with her mother; she is constantly affected by serious insecurities as a result of the lack of affection in her life; and she takes pills to help with her vocal cord injury, which will culminate in the season finale cliffhanger, with Ivy sitting in her dressing room and holding the pills, while Karen brings to a close her first stage success as Marilyn in the premiere of *Bombshell*.

We have already mentioned the episode of *Mad Men* in which Marilyn is invoked, but have still not discussed the meaning behind it:

Jacqueline Kennedy, Marilyn Monroe. Women have feelings about these women because men do. Because we want both, they want to be both. It's about how they want to be seen by us, their husbands, their boyfriends, their friends' husbands. Here's the idea, very simply. The bra is called 'The Harlequin'. In fit and form, it should be your very best. It comes in black. And white. Jackie. Marilyn. Same incredible fit, two different women. And the beauty of it is, it's the same woman. Same model.

Marilyn is a *Smash*: Depicting the Icon in NBC's Musical Drama
Raquel Crisóstomo

These words, spoken by *Mad Men*'s protagonist, advertising executive Don Draper (Jon Hamm) refer to the Playtex campaign that is the subject of the episode, but here it interests us for the way in which these two apparently opposing women are combined, in terms of class and sensuality. The vulnerable Marilyn and the mythical figure in the end come together in a single person, as occurs with the character of Ivy in her last appearance in *Smash*'s Season 1 finale, as she appears defeated in front of the bottle of pills as she sits in her dressing room.

However, we must recall that *Smash* is a musical, and therefore the songs and performances allow for the development of the different types of Marilyns put forth by the series. Therefore, not only are the songs and their lyrics significant, but so too is it necessary to consider which character performs them at a particular time. Thus, in *Smash*'s pilot, the first song Ivy sings, 'The National Pastime' – an original piece with a lighthearted tone by Marc Shaiman and Scott Wittman – also enables the viewer to imagine her onstage and see her as the natural choice for Marilyn, as Ivy herself and the casting committee can see. In fact, Ivy's songs are normally more provocative than those performed by Karen, as in the case of 'I Never Met a Wolf Who Didn't Love to Howl' (Episode 4, 'The Cost of Art', 27 February 2012) or 'Let's Be Bad' (Episode 5, 'Let's Be Bad', 5 March 2012).

On just a few occasions, Karen performs more suggestive songs, such as 'Happy Birthday Mr. President' in the pilot, which predicts the future romantic tension that arises between her and Derek, and which is repeated in the last episode (Derek to Karen: 'I do understand love'); in Karen's version of James Brown's 'It's a Man's Man's Man's World' (1966) in Episode 5; or in Derek's frustrated attempt to provide a vision of a different Marilyn through the original song 'Touch Me' (2012) written by Bonnie McKee and OneRepublic's Ryan Tedder, in which she is revealed as a victim of the creation of her own myth and her fame (Episode 8, 'The Coup', 26 March 2012):

So come and turn me on
Baby be my Marlon Brando
Take a good snapshot
Get me from my better angle
Cause I like it hot
And you know our love is scandal
Tell me what you what you waiting for?

The inclusion of this song interests us with respect to the depiction of another aspect of Marilyn, which also falls within Derek's concept for *Bombshell*: 'We all know that there's a historical Marilyn, but there's also a contemporary Marilyn, a Marilyn for a New Generation.' The director is able to see Marilyn's innocence – 'It's what Marilyn had: purity'– and at the same time, portray other aspects of her persona:

Now, if you wanna talk about Marilyn, let me tell you a couple of things [...] Yeah, Marilyn was gorgeous and wounded, but she was also a drug-addicted, a suicidal sexual icon the like of which the world cannot get enough. She is an insanely provocative and timeless figure.

Karen Cartwright is normally associated with more positive or even naive songs, such as 'Brighter than the Sun' by Colbie Caillat (Episode 7, 'The Workshop', 19 March 2012), 'Shake It Out' (2011) by Florence & The Machine (Episode 6, 'Chemistry', 12 March 2012) or 'Beautiful' by Christina Aguilera, the song with which she convinces the casting committee to hire her in Smash's pilot, identifying herself with the Marilyn who claimed that her soul was as beautiful as her body:

Every day is so wonderful
And suddenly it's hard to breathe
Now and then I get insecure
From all the fame, feel so ashamed
I am beautiful no matter what they say
Words can't bring me down
I am beautiful in every single way
Yes, words can't bring me down

The erotic icon aspect of Marilyn, as represented by Ivy, is complemented by songs that describe Marilyn's fragility, which Ivy understands very well from the various qualities that she and Marilyn share. This occurs above all in the case of 'Second-Hand White Baby Grand' (Episode 12, 'Publicity', 23 April 2012), a song which explores how the mask of fame and power that has been created is actually broken, and through it we can see Marilyn's fragility, her experiences as an orphan, and her lifelong search for approval and affection, symbolized by the song's titular second-hand white baby grand piano, a gift from her mother:

That something second-hand and broken still can make a pretty sound
Don't we all deserve a family room to live
Oh, the words can't stay unspoken until everyone has found
That Second-Hand White Baby Grand that still has something beautiful to give
I still have something beautiful to give

Furthermore, 'Let Me Be Your Star' (Marc Shaiman and Scott Wittman) becomes the theme song for Smash, sung by both stars at the end of the pilot. Karen performs the song with a need to break into the world of Broadway musicals, to which she is a

Marilyn is a *Smash*: Depicting the Icon in NBC's Musical Drama
Raquel Crisóstomo

newcomer, while Ivy is demanding a place in the spotlight that is rightfully hers, due to her extensive experience after many years in different chorus lines on Broadway. Likewise, both actresses portray the determination to become something from nothing that consumed Marilyn: 'Fade in on a girl / With a hunger for fame / With a face and a name to remember / The past fades away / Because as of this day / Norma Jeane's gone / She's moving on.' This song, originally written for *Smash*, finds its natural response in the last song closing the first season, Shaiman and Wittman's 'Don't Forget Me' ('Bombshell', Episode 15), about the price Marilyn paid for the fame for which she longed, thus restoring her position as a myth, a timeless star in the Hollywood star system, who ultimately shone because of her own merit:

> They thought they could dispose of me
> They tried to make me small
> I suffered each indignity
> But I rose above it all
> Yes, the price I paid was all I had
> But at last, I found release
> And if something good can come from bad
> The past can rest in peace [...]
> When you look to the heavens with someone you love
> And a light shining bright from afar
> Hope you see my face there
> And then offer a prayer
> And please let me be
> Let me be that star

Fig. 5: Praise for the 1983 London West End production of Marilyn! The Musical, starring Stephanie Lawrence (© Jackie Craig).

In conclusion, the interpretation of Marilyn Monroe provided by the first season of *Smash* is not a historical nor a biographical vision – in the style of those already created on other occasions in film and television – but rather, it shows the more human side of the Marilyn legend, with her foibles as well as ups and downs, above all, focusing on the magic and charm of the constructed myth itself. The Marilyn myth is examined with the respect and care required when talking about a cinema legend, as demonstrated by the following discussion between Tom – *Bombshell*'s composer – and Derek, the show's director, about Marilyn's persona and how to best, most authentically represent it onstage:

Tom: You don't get to say what she was.
Derek: Neither do you!
(*Smash*, 'The Coup')

As demonstrated by this dialogue, postmortem, Marilyn Monroe fulfilled her quest for eternal fame and celebrity, as expressed in the last verse of 'Don't Forget Me', the final song of *Smash*'s first season: 'Don't forget me... and please let me be / Let me be that star.' ●

GO FURTHER

Books
Blonde: A Novel
Joyce Carol Oates
(New York: Echo Press, 2000)

Online
Articles
'Who is the Next Marilyn Monroe? Reality Show Announced'
Ashley Lee
SheKnows.com. 12 April 2012, http://www.sheknows.com/entertainment/articles/957053/marilyn-monroe-reality-show-finding-marilyn-announced.

'How *Smash* Learned to Stop Worrying and Love the Hate-Watchers'
Denise Martin
Vulture.com. 4 February 2013,
http://www.vulture.com/2013/02/how-ismashi-learned-to-love-the-hate-watchers.html.

Films
Blonde, Andrew Dominik, dir. (United States: New Regency Pictures/Plan B Entertainment, forthcoming, 2016).

My Week with Marilyn, Simon Curtis, dir. (Great Britain: The Weinstein Company/BBC Films/Trademark Films, 2011).

The Misfits, John Huston, dir. (United States: Seven Arts Productions, 1961).

The Prince and the Showgirl, Laurence Olivier, dir. (United States: Warner Bros., 1957).

Marilyn is a *Smash*: Depicting the Icon in NBC's Musical Drama
Raquel Crisóstomo

Television
Smash, Theresa Rebeck, creator (United States: NBC, 2012–13).

The Voice, John de Moll, creator (United States: NBC, 2011–present).

Gossip Girl, Josh Safran, creator (United States: CW, 2007–12).

Mad Men, Matthew Weiner, creator (United States: AMC, 2007–present).

American Idol, Simon Fuller, creator (United States: FOX, 2002–present).

Blonde, Joyce Chopra, dir. (United States: CBS, 2001).

Musicals
Gypsy. Music by Jule Styne; lyrics by Stephen Sondheim; written by Arthur Laurents (1959). Broadway revival, Shubert Theatre (1 May 2003–20 May 2004), starring Bernadette Peters.

Hit List. Written by Drew Gasparini, Joe Iconis, Andrew McMahon, Benj Pasek and Justin Paul, Marc Shaiman and Scott Wittman, and Lucie Silvas). Version of the fictional musical of the same name in *Smash*'s second season. Performed by some members of the *Smash* cast in New York City at 54Below on 8–9 December 2013.

Marilyn! Dir. Frank Muller. Adelphi Theatre, London, 17 March – 30 July 1983.

Soundtracks
Bombshell: The New Marilyn Musical from Smash (United States: Columbia Records, 2013).
The Music of Smash (United States: Columbia Records, 2012).

'EVERYONE WANTED TO BE NEAR HER, TO TOUCH HER.'

GEORGE BARRIS,
MARILYN: NORMA JEANE

Fan Appreciation no.2
Gianandrea Colombo, *Marilyn Monroe Italia*

*Fig. 1: Gianandrea Colombo
paying homage to Marilyn
Monroe at her crypt during
the 50th Anniversary
Memorial, August 2012
(© Private Collection
Gianandrea Colombo)*

Interview by Marcelline Block

Why, when and how did you become involved with Marilyn Monroe fandom?
Hollywood classic cinema has always had a strong influence on me. I grew up watching cult films during my university years, constantly attending courses and seminars on cartoon cinema, film history and film criticism. I encountered Marilyn, completely accidentally, when I was very young. After watching the film *Bus Stop* [Joshua Logan, 1956], a remarkable performance by Marilyn playing the pale showgirl Chérie, I was stunned. Marilyn has this capacity of establishing a strong emphatic relationship with a very young audience. Marilyn's beauty and her myth, as far as I am concerned, are enclosed in that binomial of innocence and sexuality, of purity and eroticism that make her one of the most complex and vibrant creatures that cinema has ever seen. I think it is difficult to remain insensitive to the appeal of this *Magnifica Preda*. Moreover, from a critical point of view, Marilyn Monroe embodies the highest expression of a Hollywood film star and at the same time is the woman who marks the end of the star-system as a dream-generating machine. After that tragic August in 1962 cinema has begun to lose its golden aura moving towards actor and aesthetic models quite far from Marilyn's.

What is the extent of your involvement with Marilyn Monroe fandom, and which fandom communities in particular?
I am strongly involved in Marilyn Monroe fandom. For the past eighteen years, my interest and passion for this actress have grown exponentially. Much curiosity and an inborn inclination to communication allowed me to have interpersonal contacts and friendships with artists, fans and collectors all over the world. As of 2007, I have been cooperating as the PR Manager with the executive board of Some Like It Hot, a German-based international fan club set up in 1992, which is still active and growing. I have been running the online group Marilyn Monroe Italia for years – it is a small virtual community intended to create networks and contacts among people interested or keen on Marilyn in Italy and beyond, highlighting national initiatives through the exchange of precious information.

What are some highlights of your experiences with Marilyn Monroe fandom?
My passion for Marilyn has always been linked to my attitude towards collecting. For most lovers of collecting, collecting is an expression of love and devotion towards the object of their interest.
　　Personally I feel that touching and possessing something that be-

Fan Appreciation no.2
Gianandrea Colombo, *Marilyn Monroe Italia*

*Fig. 2: Marilyn Monroe's
red lipstick in a golden
case (© Private Collection
Gianandrea Colombo)
Fig. 3: Hand-painted Mexican
tile from the bath of Marilyn
Monroe's home in Brentwood,
CA where she died (© Private
Collection Gianandrea
Colombo)*

longed to Marilyn is the strongest and most significant emotional experience. A dress, a lipstick or a pair of gloves become, in fandom, something to protect and preserve, a kind of relic, a means through which you can establish the most intimate contact with Marilyn. I think this is why the value given to the material properties of Marilyn Monroe has reached, in the last auction sale, staggering figures. The preciousness and rarity of such objects make their owner a popular figure in the [fandom] community. This also goes beyond the fandom community: an heirloom that belonged to Marilyn becomes, globally, a form of investment (almost like buying a work of art) or something to be shown off as an indicator of social wealth. There are many famous people who have spent significant amounts of money buying objects belonging to Marilyn: Mariah Carey, Vanessa Paradis and finance magnate Stefano Ricucci, just to name a few.

How would you characterize the Marilyn Monroe fandom communities (a) that you are involved and (b) as a whole?
Fandom communities about Marilyn are, in my opinion, completely heterogeneous and can hardly be mapped. They involve members of different ages, activities and cultures. The Some Like It Hot fan club is surely one of the most organized among those now existing. It presents itself as a traditional club in which the member becomes an active part of the community cooperating and interacting freely without being subject to a hierarchic system. The main communication instrument is the fanzine, a print publication that is a source of updates and a means of interaction. The main objective of the fandom communities for Marilyn is to create moments of networking and sharing.

These same reasons led me to set up the Marilyn Monroe Italia online group, considering that there was no channel for Marilyn lovers into my country. An online group is very different from a traditional club. The web becomes the 'talking salon', a virtual meeting point, where personal contribution becomes precious although quite often the presence of a moderator is necessary.

How would you characterize Marilyn Monroe fandom in Europe as compared to US fandom?
I infer peculiar differences between the European fandom and the United

States fandom. In Italy, as in Europe, even if there are events, meetings and interesting private collections, the fandom is seen in a very intimate way, unlike in the States where the sharing of one's passion for Marilyn is a central dynamic in the life of the fandom community. From this perspective, it is more likely that collectors open the doors of their homes to other collectors, as the real encounter becomes a moment to make friends celebrating Marilyn and her career. Another difference I noted is a different vision of the figure of Marilyn. Without generalizing between the old and the new continent, there is a divergence of contrasting points of view. If in Europe the vision of Marilyn for the fandom is critical and objective, in the States, the idealization of the character is frequent. Thus Marilyn is elevated and idolized, forgetting that she was a human being. A beautiful woman, a vulnerable and talented actress, but a human being with virtues and faults.

How did the 50th anniversary of Marilyn Monroe's death impact (a) you personally and (b) Marilyn Monroe fandom communities at large?
The 50th anniversary of the death of Marilyn Monroe had a very strong impact. Her image was being celebrated everywhere and it is emblematic that an industry event like the Cannes Film Festival decided to choose Marilyn as its representative 'icon'. After all these years, Marilyn is more alive than ever. This is shown by the dozens of magazine covers dedicated to her, the affection and interest of the audience and the award-winning and critically acclaimed film, *My Week with Marilyn* [Simon Curtis, 2011]. Her myth is destined to endure.

What are some of the changes/new developments that you have witnessed and/or experienced in Marilyn Monroe fandom communities over the course of your involvement in them?
The Internet has definitely been the source of development and change in fandom communities.

Thanks to the world wide web, distances are truly shortened. Only fifteen years ago a fan did not have many opportunities to share his interest. The Internet was not as popular as it is today and websites were definitely less comprehensive. The fan clubs worked on a limited territory and online correspondence became the faster and more convenient form of communication. As for collecting – closely related to fandom – that was impractical. The emergence and popularity of eBay, a site that primarily targets the online collectibles niche, was a novelty allowing the web to be open equally to new prospects. Only recently did auction houses (Chris-

Fan Appreciation no.2
Gianandrea Colombo, *Marilyn Monroe Italia*

Fig. 4: Vintage classic Marilyn Monroe headshot with red ink secretarial signature and note (© Private Collection Gianandrea Colombo)

tie's, Sotheby's, Julien's...) realize the turnover of dollars that Marilyn (and a few other icons of the film and music industries) is capable of generating.

What are some new directions you envision Marilyn Monroe fandom (both yours and the larger fandom community) taking in the future? How do you see yourself involved in them?

These new directions are already underway. Facebook, Twitter and social networks in general are creating new places and ways to meet and to share specific interests. The birth a few years ago of This is Marilyn, a Marilyn-themed social network, was a turning point. The way Marilyn Monroe's popularity – even among young people – led to the creation of a social network modelled on Facebook to exchange photos and news exclusively dedicated to the diva, really makes one reflect. It is therefore necessary to integrate these new realities that mark the contemporary world.

Are you involved with any other fandom communities? If so, please discuss how these other fandom communities differ from/compare to Marilyn Monroe fandom.

Yes, I'm involved with other fandoms. Being passionate about cinema, music and theatre, collecting memorabilia and printed material, I am often in contact with other fandom communities such as Madonna's, Dalida's, Maria Callas's or James Dean's. These groups are quite similar in dynamics to those dedicated to Marilyn Monroe. Even in these cases, the object of admiration becomes a celebrity and collecting becomes a pillar of this passion. In most cases we are speaking of international artists who died prematurely. As often happens, a mysterious death feeds the myth. The only exception is Madonna – a pop icon who is still alive – and who possesses a dense crowd of admirers around the world.

What does fandom mean to you/how has fandom impacted your life? What does it mean to you to be part of a fandom community?

Being a fan, in my opinion, comes from a personal inclination, a way of being. At the same time, it is part of the educational and cultural background that accompanies each of us throughout our lives, enriching the dimension of informal learning and experience. Fandom has had a tremendous role in my life. It allowed me to meet interesting people; it led to travel, to expanding my circle of friends, to getting in contact with people connected to showbiz, to culture or to Marilyn's private life.

I believe that being part of a fandom community is the best way to share and enhance this kind of passion.

What do you think is Marilyn Monroe's ultimate legacy for her fans?
Hard to say. I often think that Marilyn – if she was still among us – could be upset by the abuse in the use of her image. She herself said, 'A sex symbol becomes a thing. I just hate to be a thing.'

Yet today her face stands out in a disrespectful way on mugs, T-shirts and many other kinds of products. Everything has been written about her, maybe even too much. Very often reality blends with fiction or fantasy. Did Marilyn Monroe have a son from JFK? Was she a Soviet spy? Did she secretly marry Fidel Castro? I don't think so. I think that in this survey, obviously confused, the duty of fans and communities is to preserve the memory and truth in an objective and sincere manner. Marilyn should be appreciated for her talent as an artist and for her sensitive soul that emerges from her personal writings recently made public, for the beauty of the pictures and for her troubled life, without continuing to torment her with unnecessary slanders. I think this is also what Norma Jeane would have wanted.

Please feel free to add more about your involvement in Marilyn Monroe fandom, such as more about your own journey to Marilyn Monroe fandom as well as your goals for your fandom: what you have achieved with it so far (such as publication, speaking and/or media engagements, leadership/ recognition within the fandom community, etc.) and what you hope to continue to achieve.
I spend a good portion of my free time participating in Marilyn Monroe fandom. This time becomes necessary, considering the ongoing cascade of news and material that daily overwhelms us. My passion leads me to store and catalogue printed material, publications, books as well as small objects that belonged to her. Thanks to the press in those days, today we can trace back exactly to facts, anecdotes and precise moments that occurred in the life of Marilyn Monroe. Undoubtedly – along with Lady Diana – she was the most photographed and followed woman in the world and her 36 years of life were consumed under the – sometimes cynical – eye of the photographic lens. Over the years, I have been able to collaborate in various fields and conduct some small interviews at a local level and for pleasure. Currently my wish is to bring Greg Thompson's play *Marilyn Forever Blonde* to Italy, which has already enthralled the US thanks to the interpretation of the beautiful Sunny Thompson. Figure 7: Gianandrea Co-

Fan Appreciation no.2
Gianandrea Colombo, *Marilyn Monroe Italia*

Fig. 5: *Gianandrea Colombo's Marilyn Monroe magazine collection (© Private Collection Gianandrea Colombo)*

Fig. 6: *Gianandrea Colombo appears on the Italian television program Storie di cinema: Marilyn (air date: 29 April 2014). Colombo was the guest of critic Tatti Sanguineti with archivist Francesca Brignoli and critic Nuccio Lodato. Here, Colombo is showing a few unpublished photos of Marilyn during her 1954 trip to Korea (the photos were taken by soldiers) (© Private Collection Gianandrea Colombo)*

Fig. 7: *Gianandrea Colombo with actress Sunny Thompson, star of Greg Thompson's play 'Marilyn Forever Blonde' (© Private Collection Gianandrea Colombo)*

lombo with actress Sunny Thompson, star of Greg Thompson's play 'Marilyn Forever Blonde' (© Private Collection Gianandrea Colombo). I have many plans for the future, some of which also involve my interest in Marilyn and cinema. Obviously, at the basis of this passion, respect and love are essential. ●

(Interview has been condensed and edited)

Biographical note
Gianandrea Colombo was born in Como, Italy. He graduated in Technologies and Communication with a focus on show business. During his studies, he successfully attended seminars and courses in journalism, creative writing, film history and film criticism. For years, he has deepened and grown a strong passion for cinema, especially for the golden era of classic Hollywood. He collects publications and memorabilia dedicated to the big-screen icons, particularly Marilyn Monroe. Lover of theatre and the cultural sphere, he is currently a freelancer in the field of Public Relations. He lives north of Milan, in the beautiful surroundings of Lake Como.

GO FURTHER

Books
L'Amore era Perduto. Un Omaggio a Marilyn
Gianandrea Colombo
(Lulu Publishing, 2012)
[See: http://www.lulu.com/spotlight/omaggio_a_marilyn.]

Plays
Marilyn Forever Blonde (written by Greg Thompson), starring Sunny Thompson: http://marilynforeverblonde.com

Online
Articles
'The Icon of the 65th Festival'

Festival de Cannes. 28 February 2012, http://www.festival-cannes.fr/en/article/58823.html.

'Marilyn Monroe Stars as the Face of the Festival de Cannes' Official Poster'
Rebecca Leffler
The Hollywood Reporter. 28 February 2012, http://www.hollywoodreporter.com/news/cannes-poster-marilyn-monroe-film-festival-295738.

Websites
MARILYN MONROE - ITALIA (Facebook group maintained by Gianandrea Colombo): https://www.facebook.com/groups/38961007734/
This is Marilyn, Social Network for Marilyn Monroe Fans: http://www.thisismarilyn.com
Some Like it Hot, International Marilyn Monroe Fan Club (Germany): http://www.marilyn-monroe-fanclub.de/english.htm

Films
My Week with Marilyn, Simon Curtis, dir. (United States: The Weinstein Company/Great Britain: BBC Films, Trademark Films, 2011).

Bus Stop, Joshua Logan, dir. (United States: Twentieth Century Fox, 1956).

River of No Return, Otto Preminger, dir. (United States: Twentieth Century Fox, 1954).

Television
Storie di cinema: Marilyn, Tatti Sanguineti, dir. (2014).
[In which Gianandrea Colombo is featured in an interview.]

Chapter
4

Marilyn Monroe's Dresses

Ange Webb

→ In his book *Dressing Marilyn: How a Hollywood Icon Was Styled by William Travilla* (2011), Andrew Hansford states that, 'costume is the second skin of the actor'.

Fig. 1: Marilyn Monroe in some of her most iconic film dresses in Love, Marilyn, ©HBO Productions, 2012.

This could apply to the film dresses of Marilyn Monroe, since some of the fan fascination with Marilyn's dresses comes from the feeling that being close to them equals being closer to her. An upsurge of popular interest in Marilyn in 2012 was partially prompted by the 50th anniversary of her death. Her life, as has often been said, was the classic rags to riches story. Audiences have been enthralled by Marilyn's vulnerability and clever charisma shining through her performances. The popularity of her dresses must also come from nostalgia for classic Hollywood glamour. Looking at the Monroe collection of dresses as a whole, there is a luxurious post-war holiday feel about them, punctuated by glitter, flower motifs and sassiness. Marilyn was so fond of her on-screen dresses that she had some of them copied and customized for her own wear. Her personal wardrobe also contained items from the top designers of her day, including Christian Dior, among others.

One of the many ways that fan devotion for Marilyn is demonstrated is by those who are willing to pay megabucks at auctions for her dresses. There were two parts to 80-year-old actress Debbie Reynolds's 2011 auctions of movie memorabilia, including Marilyn's dresses. Reynolds started collecting in 1970 when MGM auctioned off its costumes. According to Peter Bowes of BBC News, she said of the endeavour, 'I tried all these years to build a museum for the public, but I wasn't able to make my dream come true.' This made the selling of the dresses a financial necessity.

The atmosphere at both Beverly Hills auctions was electric as a rainbow of coloured gowns came under the auctioneer's hammer. Marilyn's iconic white 'subway grate' dress from *The Seven Year Itch* (Billy Wilder, 1955) was auctioned off for $4.6 million, and the red sequinned dress/feathered headdress from *Gentlemen Prefer Blondes* (Howard Hawks, 1953) fetched $1.47 million. Both were designed by William Travilla. The other two dresses that sold for high prices at this auction were the saloon costume from *River of No Return* (Otto Preminger, 1954) and the 'Heatwave' dress in *There's No Business like Show Business* (Walter Lang, 1954). The second part of the Beverly Hills 'Profiles in History' auction of 2011 was held in December of that year. This contained Marilyn's gowns from *Gentlemen Prefer Blondes* again, as well as from *Bus Stop* (Joshua Logan, 1956) and *Let's Make Love* (George Cukor, 1960). The highest price item at this auction was the William Travilla designed aubergine/grey two-piece from *Gentlemen Prefer Blondes*, which fetched $319,800.00.

Fan emotions about the white 'subway grate' Travilla dress is further shown by the New York-based 'Save the Dress' campaign of 2011, which aimed to keep that particular dress in New York, where it had its star moment in the film, as well as ensuring public access to it. inQuicity – the Manhattan entertainment technology company – and Andrew Hansford, curator of the William Travilla Estate, were behind the campaign. According to Scott Trent, quoted in an article on *DNAinfo*, 'Marilyn was very much of the people. She was an entrepreneur and formed her own production company. Despite her movie persona, she was known for taking on the studio bosses.' This yet again shows the intelligent woman who held such mystique for her fans.

Marilyn Monroe's Dresses
Ange Webb

William Travilla, a great fan of Marilyn's, showed his appreciation for her in many ways, such as by spending time with her when they exchanged pleasantries as well as in the intricacy of his personalized designs for her. Travilla designed dresses in eight Marilyn Monroe films: *Monkey Business* (Howard Hawks, 1952), *Don't Bother to Knock* (Roy Baker, 1952), *Gentlemen Prefer Blondes, How to Marry a Millionaire* (Jean Neguelsco, 1953), *There's No Business Like Show Business* (Walter Lang, 1954), *River of No Return* (Otto Preminger, 1954), *The Seven Year Itch* (Billy Wilder, 1955), and *Bus Stop* (Joshua Logan, 1956).

In Julie Burns's article 'Marilyn's Italian Style File' (2012), she gives a Travilla appreciation of Marilyn which includes his words describing her as having 'an incandescent beauty that God seldom bestows on mere mortals [...] My clothes for her were an act of love. I adored her!' When giving Travilla a nude calendar of herself, Marilyn wrote him this note: 'Billy Dear, please dress me forever. I love you, Marilyn.' Even Travilla's sketches of the dresses show an overwhelming fascination with Marilyn.

Figure 2: Suzie Kennedy wearing Marilyn Monroe's red sequined dress (designed by William Travilla) for the opening musical number of Howard Hawks's 1953 Gentlemen Prefer Blondes (© Suzie Kennedy)

In the same article about Travilla's designs, Andrew Hansford also claims that Marilyn's 'costumes were treated like couture [...] constructed from the inside out'. The dresses were always enhanced with Travilla's trademark drape or pleating and sometimes had inbuilt underwear. Marilyn's dresses sometimes had to be sewn around her as she wore them to obtain the correct tight fit. She even commissioned Travilla to design personal dresses for her.

One of the innovations that enhanced Marilyn's appeal to her contemporary fans was the introduction of widescreen cinema in 1952 with Cinerama and CinemaScope in 1953. This could increase existing cinema screen size approximately six times over and would enhance Marilyn's impact by making her appear even curvier on a curved screen. The camera lens used could incorporate a wide-angle panorama into a 35mm film. Regarding her screen presence, particularly in her white dresses, it could be said that the effect on widescreen could be excitingly suffocating to the viewer, particularly if one sat in the front row, likened to 'being smothered in baked Alaska' (according to Otis L'Guernsey, Jr). This image is quoted in Ariel Rogers's article on widescreen cinema. Rogers also describes how Marilyn's contemporary female fans might have enhanced their enjoyment by reading fan magazines of the time that detailed how to dress like Marilyn along with other lifestyle pointers, resulting in increasing the closeness between star and fan.

Creative depiction, including that of Marilyn's dresses, is one of the ways that fan

Fig. 3: Suzie Kennedy wearing Marilyn Monroe's dress for Christie's auction house (© Suzie Kennedy).

Fig. 4a/4b: Marilyn Monroe's Personal Black Silk Cocktail Dress: 'Marilyn wore this dress to an event held by the American Academy of Arts and Letters, where her husband, Arthur Miller, was recognized for receiving their Gold Medal for Drama Award on May 20, 1959 in New York City.' (Provenance: Christie's New York: The Personal Property of Marilyn Monroe, October 27–28 October 1999. Secondary: Julien's Auctions: Property from the Estate of Marilyn Monroe, 4 June 2005. Information from http://themarilynmonroecollection.com/marilyn-monroe-cocktail-dress/. (© The Scott Fortner Marilyn Monroe Collection)

affection is shown. In Roger Taylor's book *Marilyn in Art* (2006), he reveals many different types of portrayals of her dresses, including those of contemporary artists, such as Californian Ron Keas. Keas's correspondence with me indicates how his paintings pay homage to Marilyn.

In an e-mail, Ron Keas wrote that, 'because [Marilyn's] face was so beautiful […] she wanted your full attention to go to her face rather than her body. The mood of my paintings is set mainly by the colour of the dress' (e-mail correspondence, April 2012). His oil paintings are quite sensuous, and some of them are based on photographs. Ron Keas has painted Marilyn for over forty years, depicting her in many different coloured dresses, including the iconic Travilla-designed gold lamé gown Marilyn wore in *Gentlemen Prefer Blondes*. In Keas's painting *Laughing at Her Image* (1986), Marilyn wears an orange dress while she laughs at her own portrait, in which she is wearing this famous golden dress. On the back cover of *Marilyn in Art*, Marilyn herself is quoted as saying, 'We are all born sexual creatures, thank God, but it's a pity that so many people despise and crush this natural gift. Art, real art, comes from it.'

Marilyn has been featured in many different kinds of books, including comics and graphic novels, as well as those only concerned with her death. Recently there have also been books about how to make a Marilyn-style dress. It is a factor in fan phenomena that some very prestigious authors and fans include details about her dresses in their weighty volumes. This suggests intimate feelings about the actress. Michael Korda's *The Immortals* (1993) details the relationship between Marilyn Monroe, John F. Kennedy and Bobby Kennedy, set during the historical and political intrigue of that period. The novel has a stunning cast of characters, including J. Edgar Hoover, Peter Lawford, Jimmy Hoffa, Moe Dalitz, Carlos Marcello and Sam Giancana (the last three from the world of organized crime).

As part of the rich canvas of the novel, Korda gives details of several of Marilyn's dresses. There are descriptions of various different types of dresses: a tight black one; a silver grey silk; a flesh-coloured dress 'tightly moulded over her breasts and stomach' ending with a 'ruffle of beaded material' which Korda states makes Marilyn look like Venus 'emerging naked from the waves'. There are also various mentions of white dresses, which Korda says that Marilyn liked to wear, because white 'made her feel clean'. It is commonly known that Korda knew Marilyn and Bobby Kennedy well and admired them both. He, however, was not acquainted with John F. Kennedy.

Joyce Carol Oates wrote the epic novel *Blonde* (2000) about Marilyn Monroe – although apparently, she wasn't originally interested in Marilyn, but rather, in Norma

Marilyn Monroe's Dresses
Ange Webb

Fig. 5: The 'Marilyn' clothing line at the US department store Macy's features a cherry patterned dress (centre) inspired by the one worn by Marilyn's character, Roslyn Tabor, in The Misfits (John Huston, 1961) (© Macy's)

Jeane who became the celebrity later on in life. However, Oates did become a fascinated fan during the writing process, identifying with Marilyn in two ways: first, they both read and wrote, but Oates says of Marilyn, 'it all got kind of lost in the outer woman' (audio interview with Bill Goldstein, *The New York Times*, 2000). The second way that Oates identifies with Marilyn is that she felt that she had to prove herself as belonging in the world, as she describes in her interview, just as Marilyn did. A crystallization of Joyce Carol Oates's fascination with Marilyn can be seen in this description from *Blonde* of the 'subway grate' dress: 'The ivory-crepe sundress is floating and filmy as magic. The dress is magic.'

Marilyn is a muse for various artists and writers. The creation of Marilyn-inspired art – including that which depicts her dresses – feeds into the fan universe, keeping Marilyn's image alive for people who cannot get hold of any other memorabilia. It is easier and far less expensive to buy a book or poster than a genuine dress worn by and/or designed for Marilyn Monroe.

Enhancing the appeal of Marilyn's dresses to her fans was the attractiveness of her body language, which emphasized what Billy Wilder described as Marilyn's 'flesh appeal'. Marilyn read Mabel Elsworth Todd's *The Thinking Body*, which explains posture and how to show off one's bosom, along with other topics.

Marilyn read Mabel Elsworth Todd's 1938 *The Thinking Body*, which explains posture and how to show off one's bosom, along with other topics. A feature of Marilyn's style, tied in with body language, was to drop dress shoulder-straps off her shoulders. She had an early education in body language, working as a model at the 'Blue Book' model agency. Michelle Williams, star of *My Week with Marilyn* (Simon Curtis, 2011) – winner of the Golden Globe for Best Actress (musical/comedy) for her performance in this film, for which she was also nominated for the Best Actress Oscar – had to emulate Marilyn's body language for this role, according to Sara Vilkomerson of *Entertainment Weekly*. Williams describes the Monroe walk as moving 'through honey' and notes that Marilyn liked dresses that were tapered and cut off right at the knee. Fishtail dresses and strategic exposure of skin also accentuated hip movements. Williams also wore padding to encourage more swing to the hip. Some examples of Marilyn's knee-length dresses are the diaphanous Orry-Kelly dresses from *Some Like it Hot* and Roslyn's cherry dress in *The Misfits* (John Huston, 1961).

Marilyn's attractive body language also comes through in photo shoots such as Milton Greene's 'The Red Sitting' (January 1957). Greene was a New Yorker whose work was featured in many influential American magazines in the 1950s and 1960s. After meeting Marilyn in 1953, they became friends and formed their own film production company. Marilyn's frothy/satiny red dress in these photos emphasizes her playful languour. The dress's halter neck emphasizes the classic, lusted-after Monroe pose: blonde head tilted up, eyes with enquiring eyebrows looking down over parted lips.

Fig. 6: Immortal Marilyn
Fan Club's Jackie Craig and
Leah Peterson with Marilyn
impersonator Suzie Kennedy
(centre) at Seward Johnson's
'Forever Marilyn' statue (2011)
when it was in Palm Springs,
CA in 2013. Johnson's
'Forever Marilyn' recreates
Marilyn's iconic pose in William Travilla's 'subway grate'
dress from The Seven Year
Itch. (©Jackie Craig, 2013)

Despite the substantial change in women's body shapes since Marilyn's time, there is still a great fan demand for wearing imitation dresses of hers. According to Sean Poulter in a 2011 *Daily Mail* article, taking British women as an example, one in two fall into the 'rectangular' category, which means there is only a minor difference between bust, waist and hip measurements. 'Alvanon', the clothing fit analysts, discovered this fact recently. Marilyn Monroe was always an hourglass shape, which accounts for about one in ten British women. Her usual measurements were as follows: bust: 35–37 inches; waist: 22–23 inches and hips: 35–36 inches. Despite the change from the hourglass to the rectangular shape of contemporary women, there is still a great demand for visual representations of women in Marilyn-type dresses, which creates business for vintage stores and dressmakers.

There are many celebrity fans of Marilyn who like to feel close to her by imitating or wearing similar clothes. Among these fans are Madonna, Lindsey Lohan and Scarlett Johansson. Some of the celebrities who wear Marilyn clone dresses are not always hourglass shaped. The dresses that seem popular for celebrities to copy are the Marilyn white dresses including the 'subway grate' dress and the pink dress from *Gentlemen Prefer Blondes* (from the musical number 'Diamonds Are a Girl's Best Friend' by Jule Styne and Leo Robin, 1949), also designed by William Travilla. It seems that celebrities often perform Marilyn's rendition of 'Happy Birthday Mr. President', such as American singer Lana Del Rey at the start of the video for her song 'National Anthem' (2012). The stars that wear Marilyn dresses also reportedly pay homage to her in other ways: Britney Spears often visits Marilyn's grave; Nicole Kidman yearns to have Marilyn-like curves; Paris Hilton named her dog after Marilyn; and former Spice Girl Gerri Halliwell enjoys watching her father's copies of Marilyn films.

Some performers have made a career out of being Marilyn lookalikes, such as Susan Griffiths and Rachael Le Roque. Possibly the best-known Marilyn lookalike is Suzie Kennedy [Editor's note: see the interviews with Griffiths and Kennedy in this volume]. According to the Classique Promotions website, Suzie Kennedy knows everything that there is to know about Marilyn and is probably Marilyn's 'biggest fan'. She owns replicas of many of Marilyn's screen dresses including the 'subway grate' dress, the gold lamé dress and the *Niagara* (Henry Hathaway, 1953) one. Suzie Kennedy has also modelled dresses for Christie's and Bonhams auctioneers. She has modelled for the William Travilla estate and the memorabilia collector David Gainsborough Roberts.

There are many vintage shops and sites worldwide where it is possible for a Marilyn fan to purchase a dress in the style of their idol. Many vintage clothing websites have

Marilyn Monroe's Dresses
Ange Webb

Fig. 7: Marilyn fan Megan Owen at the March 2012 Getty Gallery Exhibit in London standing next to Marilyn Monroe's costumes and dresses from Gentlemen Prefer Blondes (Howard Hawks, 1953) and There's No Business like Show Business (Walter Lang, 1954). (©Megan Owen)

their own blogs, including *Fancy Dress Ball*, which does a Marilyn-style white dress. Some of the vintage shops in the United Kingdom are reminiscent of 1960s boutiques, which give off a psychedelic vibe, although, with their websites and blogs, they are thoroughly multimedia-equipped for the twenty-first century. Some of them have a big Marilyn Monroe interest. Amongst them, 'Second Hand Rose' in Worcester was particularly fascinating, as it employed a model named Holly Dolly who 'loves' Marilyn and works as her lookalike for events (after eight years in Worcester's Hopmarket, as of June 2014, the store transitioned to becoming a primarily online retailer). Birmingham has an arts events space called The Custard Factory, which houses the Le Keux Vintage Salon, where fans can buy Marilyn-type dresses or make an appointment for a Marilyn Monroe makeover.

Vintage fashion blogs abound today, including many devoted to Marilyn's dresses. Some provide tips on how to dress like her, while others express admiration for her. *Sammy Davis Vintage* is particularly noteworthy, as it displays screen shots from some of Sammy's – the site's author – favourite Marilyn movies. These images are followed by a link to the Etsy vintage website where you can buy a similar Marilyn outfit (which includes her dresses). *Hel Looks* is a street-style blog from Helsinki, started in 2005, detailing various individual looks, among which is featured a photo of 23-year-old Emilia, who states that 'classic Marilyn Monroe is my style icon'. Shona Daly, who runs *The Prim Girl* blog, also owns a vintage clothing store in Norwich, which features 1980s fashion alongside the 'typical 50's feminine iconic silhouette'. There is a very affectionate recent piece on the blog about Marilyn's dresses, which describes the latest Marilyn exhibit in London (Getty Images Gallery, 2012). Much attention is paid to how Marilyn had to be carefully fitted into her dresses, prompted by an observation of the cut of the dresses in the exhibition. There are also intimate details concerning the wear and tear of the dresses, including underarm sweat marks. *Prim Girl* describes Marilyn as being 'a perfect shape to fulfil the dresses of her era!'

The contemporary blogs mentioned above are only a small sampling of those that are universally available. They are therapeutic for fans of Marilyn in many ways: they share information/emotions, they keep memories alive for another generation, and they are a chance to show off wannabe dresses. The 'Marilyn Monroe Goddess' section of *Becky's Treasures* stands out among many Marilyn websites, as Becky is a fan who has been collecting everything Marilyn for a long time, including paper dolls that one can dress up. Her representations of Marilyn's dresses include wallpapers, e-cards and an art gallery.

Vintage shops are excellent sources for fans to find Marilyn-type dresses. However, how does one know if he or she has come across an original Marilyn Monroe dress? David Gainsborough Roberts, the owner of what is perhaps the largest private collection of Marilyn dresses, provides a few answers, as mentioned in *Paul Fraser Collectibles*:

- Ask where the dresses came from
- The dresses from the films have a tag number on the back, which has a corresponding number in the film studio records
- Textile experts will let you know if the type of material used in the dress is the type of fabric that would have been around in Marilyn's era

In the same article, Gainsborough Roberts says that of all of Marilyn's dresses, the dress he would most like to own is the iconic 'subway grate' white dress. A little bronze ballerina toy of Marilyn's is also mentioned, which she had in the orphanage, and which she used to illustrate the point to the other girls that she wanted to be famous when she grew up! It brings to mind the affectionate ballerina photographs of Milton Greene, which famously depict Marilyn in a tutu.

The final dress that Marilyn wore was a green Pucci with a green chiffon scarf. This was the outfit in which she was laid to rest at her funeral on 8 August 1962 at Westwood village mortuary chapel. This was a favourite outfit that she had worn at a press conference in Mexico City earlier that year. In her hands was a posy of pink teacup roses, a gift from her ex-husband Joe DiMaggio. Graham McCann sums up fan feeling about Marilyn and her dresses in a poignant sentence from his book, *Marilyn Monroe: The Body in the Library* (1988): 'We imitate, reproduce, publish and speculate in one mass rescue fantasy because we cannot bear […] to see her leave over that last, lost horizon.' ●

GO FURTHER

Books
Marilyn in Fashion: The Enduring Influence of Marilyn Monroe
Christopher Nickens and George Zeno
(Philadelphia: Running Press, 2012)

Dressing Marilyn: How a Hollywood Icon Was Styled by William Travilla
Andrew Hansford
(London: Goodman Books, 2011)

Marilyn in Art
Roger Taylor
(London: Pop Art Books, 2006)

Marilyn Monroe's Dresses
Ange Webb

Hollywood Costume Design by Travilla
Maureen E. Lynn Reilly
(Atglen, PA: Schiffer Publishing, 2003)

Blonde
Joyce Carol Oates
(London: Fourth Estate, 2000)

Milton's Marilyn: The Photographs of Milton H. Greene
Milton H. Greene
(Germany: Schirmer/Mosel Verlag Gmbh, 1998)

The Immortals
Michael Korda
(London: Pan Books, 1993)

Marilyn Monroe: The Body in the Library
Graham McCann
(Cambridge: Polity, 1988)

Mystique and Identity: Women's Fashions of the 1950s
Barbara A. Schreier
(Norfolk, VA: Chrysler Museum, 1984)

The Thinking Body
Mabel Elsworth Todd
(New York and London: P.B. Hoeber, 1937)

Extracts/Essays/Articles
'Smothered in baked Alaska: The Anxious Appeal of Widescreen Cinema'
Ariel Rogers
Cinema Journal. 51: 3 (2012), pp. 74–86.

Online
Articles
'The Vintage Dresses of Miss Marilyn Monroe.' *The Prim Girl.* 9 May 2012, http://www.theprimgirl.com/2012/05/09/the-vintage-dresses-of-miss-marilyn-monroe/.

'Marilyn's Italian Style File'
Julie Burns

Italy Magazine. 6 February 2012, www.italymagazine.com/featured-story/marilyns-italian-style-file.

'Debbie Reynolds: I'll Perform Until I Kick It'
Peter Bowes
BBC.com. 29 November 2011, http://www.bbc.com/news/entertainment-arts-15918755.

'The Magic of Marilyn Monroe'
Jess Cartner-Morley
The Guardian. 15 November 2011, http://www.theguardian.com/fashion/2011/nov/15/marilyn-monroe-film-costume-designer.

'Holiday Preview: Michelle Williams'
Sara Vilkomerson
Entertainment Weekly. 11 November 2011, www.ew.com/ew/article/0,,20545940,00.html.

'Marilyn Monroe Fans Want to Bring Iconic Dress to NYC'
Amy Zimmer
DNAInfo. 2 June 2011, http://www.dnainfo.com/new-york/20110602/murray-hill-gramercy/marilyn-monroe-fans-want-bring-iconic-dress-nyc.

'Marilyn Monroe Hourglass Figure? British Women are More Likely to be a Rectangle'
Sean Poulter
Daily Mail. 28 May 2011, http://www.dailymail.co.uk/femail/article-1391671/Hourglass-No-shapes-like-rectangle.html.

'It's a Dog's Life, Beverly Hills Style: Paris Hilton Reveals Her Pampered Pooches' Kennel Mansion'
Daily Mail. 8 June 2009, http://www.dailymail.co.uk/tvshowbiz/article-1191579/Its-dogs-life-Beverly-Hills-style-Paris-Hilton-reveals-pampered-pooches-kennel-mansion.html.

'Last Talk With a Lonely Girl: Marilyn Monroe'
Richard Meryman
The Guardian. 14 September 2007 (edited version; first published in *Life* magazine, 17 August 1962), http://www.theguardian.com/theguardian/2007/sep/14/greatinterviews.

'Audio Interview: Joyce Carol Oates'
Bill Goldstein

Marilyn Monroe's Dresses
Ange Webb

The New York Times. 28 March 2000,
http://www.nytimes.com/books/00/04/02/specials/oates.html.

'David Gainsborough Roberts Monroe Collection Interview: Marilyn is Probably the Best Investment.' Paul Fraser Collectibles (n.d.), http://www.paulfrasercollectibles. com/section.asp?catid=179&docid=6224.

Websites
Macy's Marilyn Monroe Collection: http://www1.macys.com/shop/juniors-clothing/ marilyn-monroe?id=63017
Classique Promotions: Marilyn Monroe (Suzie Kennedy):
http://www.classiquepromotions.co.uk/7/64/Marilyn+Monroe
Second Hand Rose Vintage Worcester: http://secondhandroseworcester.co.uk/
Sammy Davis Vintage: http://sammydvintage.com/
Etsy Vintage: www.etsy.com/category/vintage
Hel Looks: www.hel-looks.com
The Prim Girl Blog: http://theprimgirl.wordpress.com/?s=marilyn+monroe&submit=Search
Paul Fraser Collectibles: www.paulfrasercollectibles.com/
Becky's Treasures ('Marilyn Monroe Goddess'): http://www.angelfire.com/ny/ BECKYSTREASURES/index.html
Rachael Le Roque: http://www.saatchiart.com/Rachaelleroque
Oil Paintings of Marilyn Monroe by Ron Keas (including 'Laughing at Her Image'): http://www.monroepaintings.com
David Gainsborough Roberts' collections: http://en.wikicollecting.org/david-gainsborough-roberts-collections#toc1
Assorted Marilyn Art: http://www.immortalmarilyn.com/MarilynArt.html
William Travilla's Marilyn Monroe: http://www.marilynmonroe.ca/camera/galleries/ costumes/travilla/
The Costumes:
http://www.marilynmonroe.ca/camera/galleries/costumes/
LeKeux Vintage Salon: http://www.lekeuxvintagesalon.co.uk

Films
My Week with Marilyn, Simon Curtis, dir. (Great Britain: Pinewood Studio, 2011).

Let's Make Love, George Cukor, dir. (United States: Twentieth Century Fox, 1960).

Some Like It Hot, Billy Wilder, dir. (United States: United Artists, 1959).

Bus Stop, Joshua Logan, dir. (United States: Twentieth Century Fox, 1956).

The Seven Year Itch, Billy Wilder, dir. (United States: Twentieth Century Fox, 1955).

River of No Return, Otto Preminger, dir. (United States: Twentieth Century Fox, 1954).

There's No Business like Show Business, Walter Lang, dir. (United States: Twentieth Century Fox, 1954).

Gentleman Prefer Blondes, Howard Hawks, dir. (United States: Twentieth Century Fox, 1953).

How to Marry a Millionaire, Jean Neguelsco, dir. (United States: Twentieth Century Fox, 1953).

Don't Bother to Knock, Roy Baker, dir. (United States: Twentieth Century Fox, 1952).

Monkey Business, Howard Hawks, dir. (United States: Twentieth Century Fox, 1952).

Songs
'National Anthem'
Lana Del Rey
In Lana Del Rey, *Born to Die* (Interscope Records/Polydor Records/Stranger Records, 2012).
[Video: https://www.youtube.com/watch?v=sxDdEPEDOh8.]

Conferences
Who Designed Marilyn's Dress? Impact, Craft, and Future of Film Costume, New York University, Department of Art and Art Professions/Costume Studies, 10 May 2014, http://steinhardt.nyu.edu/art/costume/conference2014.

Exhibits
'Marilyn', Getty Images Gallery, London, 9 March–23 May 2012, http://www.gettyimagesgallery.com/exhibitions/archive/marilyn.aspx.

Fan Appreciation no.3
Scott Fortner, The Marilyn Monroe Collection

Figure 1: Scott Fortner with some of the items in his Marilyn Monroe collection. Fortner, who is highly active in the MM fandom community, has amassed one of the largest private collections of Marilyn Monroe memorabilia. (Photograph by Yury Toroptsov).

Interview by Marcelline Block

Figure 2: Marilyn Monroe's Personal Mink Fur Collar: 'Marilyn wore this fur regularly in New York City, and during at least two Milton Greene photo shoots.. She's pictured wearing the collar on other occasions, including in England when filming The Prince and The Showgirl.' Provenance: Christie's New York: The Personal Property of Marilyn Monroe, October 27-28, 1999. http:// themarilynmonroecollection. com/marilyn-monroe-mink-fur-collar/ (© From The Scott Fortner Marilyn Monroe Collection)

'I didn't pick Marilyn, I think she picked me': My interest in Marilyn began very early on, and I started collecting Marilyn-related memorabilia when I was actually quite young. I don't even remember the first time I saw a Marilyn Monroe photo or movie. I've just been fascinated by her for as long as I can remember. Many people can remember the very first time they encountered Marilyn, whether on the big screen, or perhaps a photograph of her. Unfortunately, I don't have my own recollection. I was recently asked, 'Why Marilyn? Why this icon instead of someone else?' My immediate response was, 'I didn't pick Marilyn, I think she picked me.'

A labour of love: My involvement with Marilyn Monroe fandom is rather extensive. As the owner of one of the largest private collections of Marilyn Monroe memorabilia, I've become fairly well known in the community. I'm closely associated with *Marilyn Remembered*, which is the longest-running fan club in existence today, and I'm a key member of the club's operations staff. We sponsored the 50th Anniversary Memorial Service for Marilyn Monroe, and it was very well attended by fans from around the globe. I played a significant role in planning, organizing and implementing the 50th anniversary memorial service for Marilyn. It was truly a labour of love. An incredible amount of work, but all done for the benefit of Marilyn and the Marilyn Monroe community the world over. I always find it extremely intriguing when

Fan Appreciation no.3
Scott Fortner, The Marilyn Monroe Collection

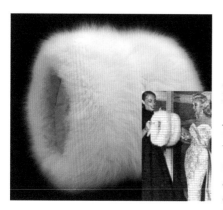

Figure 3: Marilyn Monroe's Personal White Fox Fur Muff: 'White fox fur muff with white satin lining, which Marilyn wore to the premiere of How To Marry A Millionaire, November 14, 1953.' Provenance: Christie's New York: The Personal Property of Marilyn Monroe, October 27-28, 1999. http://themarilynmonroecollection.com/marilyn-monroe-white-fox-muff/ (© From The Scott Fortner Marilyn Monroe Collection)

I sit back and take note of just how popular Marilyn Monroe is now. I think, 'Where have you been? Are you all just catching up with the rest of us now?' Or, perhaps people are just able to be much more public via online resources such as Facebook, Twitter and Tumblr, etc. Regardless, Marilyn Monroe is more popular today than she's ever been. I'm also a member of another Marilyn Monroe club, Immortal Marilyn, and I sponsor an online Marilyn Monroe forum, Everlasting-Star.

It's all about the fandom: Without a doubt, the greatest highlight of being associated with other fans of Marilyn Monroe is the fans themselves. Not surprisingly, Marilyn's appeal is worldwide, and with that I've developed strong relationships with people from all over the world, and in many cases I consider these people to be my extended family. Another highlight is actually meeting people who knew Marilyn personally. It's so interesting to hear stories about this woman from people who encountered her either personally or professionally. She's become such an icon that in some ways it's easy to forget that she was a real person, so to talk with people who spent time with Marilyn Monroe is an exceptional experience. Other highlights of being associated with Marilyn Monroe fandom include sharing my knowledge of and respect for Marilyn via interviews, news reports and documentaries, being photographed as part of a Marilyn Monroe focused photo essay with my portrait being exhibited in Paris, speaking about Marilyn in front of large audiences, and experiencing the privilege of exhibiting items from collection at the Academy of Motion Picture Arts and Sciences in Los Angeles. Being a fan of Marilyn Monroe is an eternally enriching experience. I've made some wonderful friends, many of whom I now consider my family, and we all have this amazing woman in common. Establishing and maintaining these relationships is very important. We share our lives, our triumphs and our struggles, and this often goes way beyond the Marilyn Monroe connection. While she's the glue that holds us all together, we've also developed deep and meaningful relationships that will hopefully last a lifetime. With the advancement of technology and online resources, the Marilyn Monroe community has grown beyond traditional fan clubs. Today, with the Internet, and online forums, Twitter and Facebook, fans across the globe

Figure 4 and Figure 5: Marilyn Monroe's Pucci Blouse: From the 1999 Christie's Auction, The Personal Property of Marilyn Monroe, a lime green, long-sleeved boat neck Pucci blouse, silk jersey, size 14, label reads, Emilio Pucci / Florence Italy and Made in Italy exclusively for Saks Fifth Avenue. 'The blouse Marilyn wore when rehearsing for her performance of 'Happy Birthday Mr. President' for President John F. Kennedy, Madison Square Garden on May 19, 1962. Also the blouse Marilyn wore when the last photos of her alive were taken on July 28 & 29, 1962, at the Cal-Neva Lodge in Lake Tahoe, Nevada.' http:// themarilynmonroecollection. com/marilyn-monroe-pucci-blouse/ (© The Scott Fortner Marilyn Monroe Collection)

can connect with each other to discuss Marilyn, and share photographs, ideas and opinions. It's really quite extraordinary how Marilyn brings so many people together from different cultures and societies. I see the Marilyn Monroe community continuing to grow, in particular via the Internet. It's so much easier today to connect with fans from every country. I've connected with people all over the world, just chatting about Marilyn and the impact she continues to have. The fascination with Marilyn can't be described. On a personal and intimate scale we all connect with her in our own special way, and it's different for each person. We relate to Marilyn because we experience many of the same challenges she did. On a broader level, Marilyn will always be the quintessential Hollywood glamour queen and sex symbol. She will be eternally young and beautiful, shrouded in mystery and tragedy.

Keeping the Legend Alive as a Collector of Marilyn Monroe-owned items: My personal journey with Marilyn has been extremely rewarding and fulfilling. I'm quite lucky to be in the position I'm in, specifically that of a collector of Marilyn Monroe-owned items. I'm thrilled to be able to share my collection with fans around the world via exhibitions and shows. Marilyn's draw is quite powerful, and fans truly enjoy seeing up-close and personal the items that she wore and held, books from her library, her handwriting, etc. It's a wonderful way to experience the woman behind the celebrity. I've exhibited the collection for charitable purposes in the past, and that was a very rewarding experience for me. All proceeds from the fundraising events were used for children's services. Marilyn

Fan Appreciation no.3
Scott Fortner, The Marilyn Monroe Collection

Figure 6: Marilyn Monroe's Evening Cape: 'Pastel yellow, green and beige silk evening cape, in a brocade pattern depicting roses and leaves. Worn during one of Marilyn's most glamorous appearances: The premiere of the James Dean film East of Eden in New York City, March 9, 1955. This cape to have been sold at the 1999 Christie's Auction: The Personal Property of Marilyn Monroe. Two Christie's tags still pinned to the garment. Item sold at the 2005 Julien's Auction: Property from The Estate of Marilyn Monroe.' http://themarilynmonroecollection.com/marilyn-monroe-evening-cape/ (© From The Scott Fortner Marilyn Monroe Collection)

Figure 7: Marilyn Monroe's Personal Overcoat: Worn by Marilyn 'as she exited Polyclinic Hospital, July 11, 1961, following gallbladder surgery.' Provenance: Christie's New York: The Personal Property of Marilyn Monroe, October 27-28, 1999. http://themarilynmonroecollection.com/marilyn-monroe-personal-overcoat/ (© From The Scott Fortner Marilyn Monroe Collection)

loved children so I wanted to give to a cause that she would support. I've been lucky enough to present on the topic of Marilyn Monroe in front of large audiences, which was also very rewarding for me. As far as what I hope to continue to achieve, I'd like to continue to share my collection with the world, giving fans across the globe the opportunity to get a glimpse of the woman behind the movie star, which is the side of Marilyn that I find the most interesting. She was undeniably a glamorous movie star, but there was a real person behind the film costumes and the premieres, behind the thousands of photographs, and the celebrity gossip. I want people to get to know the intimate side of Marilyn.

She offered us so much more than what we saw on the silver screen, and what Hollywood took from her. She was a complex and talented woman. I'd also like to continue philanthropic work by showing my collection at future fundraising events. But most important, I'll continue to 'keep the legend alive' by meeting new fans, writing about Marilyn on my blog, continuing to collect, and following my passion. •

(Answers have been condensed and edited)

~~~~~~~~~~~~~~~

GO FURTHER

Online
Websites
Scott Fortner's The Marilyn Monroe Collection: http://themarilynmonroecollection.com/
Scott Fortner's blog: http://www.themarilynmonroecollection.blogspot.com
Scott Fortner's tour of Marilyn's last home:
http://themarilynmonroecollection.blogspot.com/2010/07/my-tour-of-marilyns-last-home.html
Scott Fortner's Marilyn Monroe collection: http://en.wikicollecting.org/scott-fortner-s-marilyn-monroe-collection
Marilyn Remembered: http://www.marilynremembered.org
Immortal Marilyn: http://www.immortalmarilyn.com
Everlasting-Star: http://www.everlasting-star.net

Social Media
The Marilyn Monroe Collection Facebook fan page:
https://www.facebook.com/TheMarilynMonroeCollection
Twitter: @MMCollection

Television
Love, Marilyn, Documentary, Liz Garbus, dir.
(United States: HBO Productions, 2012).
With Her, Laurent Morlet, dir (France: Laurent Morlet Productions, 2012).
[Includes statements and interviews with Scott Fortner.]

Fan Appreciation no.3
Scott Fortner, The Marilyn Monroe Collection

Exhibits

The Marilyn Monroe Collection, travelling exhibit: http://
themarilynmonroecollection.com/the-marilyn-monroe-exhibits/
The Marilyn Monroe Collection at the Oscars (in October 2011, Scott
Fortner was a guest of the Academy of Motion Picture Arts and
Sciences, where he spoke in the Linwood Dunn Theater as part of
'Hollywood Home Movies III : Treasures from the Academy Film Archive
Collection'): https://www.facebook.com/media/set/?set=a.40179076316
4351.99566.119074018102695&type=3&l=3ce81a672f.
Hollywood Home Movies III: Treasures from the Academy Film Archive
Collection: http://www.oscars.org/events-exhibitions/events/2011/10/
hollywood-home.html

'SHE WAS – AND STILL IS – THE SUPERNOVA OF AMERICAN POSTWAR CELEBRITIES AGAINST WHICH ALL OTHERS ARE MEASURED.'

RICHARD B. WOODWARD

Chapter
5

Performing Marilyn: Michelle Williams in *My Week with Marilyn*

Zachary Ingle

→ Why has Marilyn Monroe, one of the most iconic Hollywood stars, been portrayed so often in cinema and television? The same cannot be said of other legendary figures of cinema such as John Wayne, Cary Grant, Jimmy Stewart, Audrey Hepburn or Humphrey Bogart. Maybe it is because Marilyn was almost a caricature, but was she any more so than Wayne?

Fig. 1: The film narrates the time Colin Clark (Eddie Redmayne), while working for the first time as a production assistant on a film, spent with Marilyn Monroe (Williams) during the making of Sir Laurence Olivier's The Prince and the Showgirl. Clark's eponymous memoir was adapted to screen as My Week with Marilyn (© The Weinstein Company.

In *My Week with Marilyn* (Simon Curtis, 2011), Kenneth Branagh plays another icon, Sir Laurence Olivier, but that is not much of a stretch for him, since Branagh's entire career seems to have been modelled after Olivier's – even if the idea of Sir Laurence directing *Thor* (2011) seems far-fetched. Of course, a slew of Elvis Presley impersonators have arisen since The King's death in 1977, despite his almost unparalleled iconic status. Certain actors have even made their careers based on performing Marilyn, such as Susan Griffiths, who has played Marilyn or a Marilyn looka-like in almost all of her television and film appearances, perhaps most famously in the 1950s diner Jack Rabbit Slims in *Pulp Fiction* (Quentin Tarantino, 1994) [Editor's note: see interview with Susan Griffiths elsewhere in this volume]. Discussing another actress 'performing Marilyn' may strike some readers as odd, particularly since Marilyn – rather, Norma Jeane – herself constantly needed to do the same. Indeed, *My Week with Marilyn* certainly hints at this, when Marilyn transforms into *Marilyn*, wowing the Windsor Castle staff.

My Week with Marilyn, based on both of Colin Clark's diaries (*The Prince, the Show-girl, and Me* and *My Week with Marilyn*), is a faithful adaptation of both books. First published in 1995, Clark's *The Prince, the Showgirl, and Me* is a production diary that covers not only the shooting of *The Prince and the Showgirl* (Laurence Olivier, 1957) from 7 August to 17 November 1956, but also how Clark obtained the job and his pre-production work, with entries dating back to 3 June. The book *My Week with Marilyn*, not published until 2000, only focuses on the week of 11–19 September 1956 (largely missing in the earlier account), which serves as the heart of the film as well. In the film, Colin (Eddie Redmayne) adores Marilyn (Michelle Williams), which contrasts with Clark's original impressions of her as recounted in *The Prince, the Showgirl, and Me* in which he notes that, 'Her figure […] is fantastic but a little on the plump side' and that she has 'too much fakery: peroxide hair, dead white make-up, heavy lipstick, but that is her image' (p. 174). His critical comments when she arrives at the studio for a screen test, lacking make-up, seem almost malicious; he describes her as having a 'nasty complexion' with 'a lot of facial hair' (p. 177). His opinions in *The Prince, the Showgirl, and Me* do not really change after that magical week in September, as he and the film's crew became increasingly frustrated with Marilyn's behaviour. The 5 November entry has a definite mean-spirited-ness about it: 'Guy Fawkes night, and no prizes for guessing where we would like to plant a bomb. But she didn't turn up at all this morning, so we had a relatively peaceful day' (p. 292). Yet the comparison between *My Week with Marilyn* and *The Prince, the Showgirl, and Me* is not a simple 'Jekyll and Hyde' account of the same events. Clark does include

Performing Marilyn: Michelle Williams in *My Week with Marilyn*
Zachary Ingle

flattering comments about Marilyn in *The Prince, the Showgirl, and Me*. When comparing her to beauty Maxine Audley (who has a small role in *The Prince and the Showgirl*), Clark notes, 'For all the pills and problems, MM looks so full of life and *joie de vivre* in comparison' (p. 281).

The film's reference to Marilyn's lack of discipline as an actor, from arriving hours late on set to forgetting her lines, is described in Clark's journal:

> MM doesn't really forget her lines. It is more as if she had never quite learnt them – as if they are pinned to her mental noticeboard so loosely that the slightest puff of wind will send them floating to the floor [...] She can be in mid-speech, and then she gives a little frown, her lips part, her eyes look puzzled, and she stops. She doesn't say 'Oh drat, what is the next line?' or anything. She just stops [...] Even if MM does have another try before the camera stops running, she is too flustered and her eyes are glazed. (p. 213)

Fig. 2: Newlyweds Marilyn Monroe (Michelle Williams) and Arthur Miller (Dougray Scott) in My Week with Marilyn *(© The Weinstein Company)*

A turning point in Clark's opinion toward Marilyn occurred, appropriately enough, because of her breathtaking body. He admits that 'she went up in my estimation' the day that he barged into her dressing room and accidentally discovered her completely nude. Yet it was not just her sexual allure that changed his mind, but rather her response ('Oh Colin. And you an old Etonian!') that revealed more intelligence than she had previously let on. (In the film, this line is reserved for Colin's embarrassing erection after emerging from the skinny dip.) The cinematic Colin seems to be interested in Marilyn at a much earlier stage, indeed seeing her in a cinema in the opening scene. This stands in contrast to the book, where he admits to preferring younger, thinner women (like then 18-year-old Susan Strasberg, daughter of Marilyn's acting coach Paula Strasberg) over those with more voluptuous bodies such as Marilyn.

Fig. 3: Fig. 2: Newlyweds Marilyn Monroe (Michelle Williams) and Arthur Miller (Dougray Scott) in My Week with Marilyn *(© The Weinstein Company)*

Despite this faithfulness to the books, the film does not truly capture, however, Marilyn's declining mental health and addictions, which Clark elaborates on in his production diary. Notwithstanding Marilyn's growth as an actor as a result of her experience in England, *The Prince and the Showgirl* can be considered the beginning of the end of her life and her career. Her marriage to Arthur Miller got off to a rocky start, and her tardiness and generally unprofessional behaviour would become increasingly worse on the sets of her later films *Some Like It Hot* (Billy Wilder, 1959), *The Misfits* (John Huston, 1961) and the unfinished *Something's Got to Give* (George Cukor, 1962). Clark complains about the uppers and downers she constantly took and their effects on her: 'But now she is like a see-saw, forever being pushed up or down and never level. In the end she will loop the loop like her mum' (p. 258). More damning are his comments about her drug abuse:

The trouble is that she takes extra pills when she doesn't feel 100%, without really knowing what effects the pills will have […] She just takes another pill to counteract the first one. As a result she was at her most distant and remote. When she is like that, no one can talk to her […] This is so sad, because she should be on top of the world […] MM looks more and more vulnerable and I am sorry for her. But when a whole studio is waiting to do an expensive and complicated shot, going ga-ga is not the way to be popular. (p. 287)

Depicting such self-destructive conduct would surely have changed the tenor of the film.

The general opinion toward Marilyn on the set did not lighten up after filming and post-synchronization were completed: 'We knew we would never see her again and, sad to tell, it was an immense relief' (p. 304). According to Clark's last diary entry, Marilyn gave every member of the crew a bottle (presumably of wine) or a leather purse. They promptly threw them in the rubbish bin. (According to director Simon Curtis's DVD commentary, this scene was cut from the film as it would have been detrimental to the film's portrayal of Marilyn.) Clark closes with, 'I expect we will all recover. But it's going to take a long time' (p. 306).

Neither the books nor the film touch on the two main reasons why Sir Laurence Olivier, who initially had fallen in love with Marilyn so much that he just had to make a film with her, had cooled off in his passions toward her: first, Marilyn's recent marriage to Miller; and second, the fact that Olivier's wife Vivien Leigh had just become pregnant, sparking his interest in a marriage about which he had recently felt lackadaisical. The film and books take more pleasure in emphasizing Olivier's conflicts with Marilyn over the Method approach to acting and her reliance on Paula Strasberg, resulting in what was, in Olivier's perspective, an extra director on the set.

Watching *The Prince and the Showgirl* today reveals little of the problems the film went through in production: Marilyn's unprofessional behaviour; Strasberg on the set; Miller making life difficult for Marilyn; and being based on a mediocre Terence Rattigan play to begin with. The viewer can hardly detect the planned long takes that Clark's production diary mentions, which Olivier, making his first non-Shakespearean film, had to break up because Marilyn too often forgot her lines. It definitely is one of Marilyn's most assured performances and has its rightful place in a string of her films (*Bus Stop* [Joshua Logan, 1956], *Some Like It Hot*, *The Misfits*) that showed her true potential as a comedic and dramatic actress. For this surprising performance in *The Prince and the Showgirl*, Marilyn received a Laurel Award nomination, as well as a BAFTA nomination for Best Foreign Actress.

The critics lauded Marilyn's performance. Archer Winsten of the *New York Post* praised her performance, stating,

Performing Marilyn: Michelle Williams in *My Week with Marilyn*
Zachary Ingle

Marilyn Monroe [...] has never seemed more in command of herself as a person and comedienne. She manages to make her laughs without sacrificing the real Marilyn to play-acting. This, of course, is something one can expect from great, talented and practiced performers. It comes as a most pleasant surprise from Marilyn Monroe, who has been half-actress, half-sensation.

A *Los Angeles Times* reviewer labeled it 'Miss Monroe's best cinema effort' and credited her director as 'she reveals a real sense of comedy'. *The New York Herald Tribune* admired her turn, particularly in such an unsubstantial role that

Fig. 4/4a: Marilyn Monroe (Michelle Williams) performs the song and dance number 'Heat Wave' in the opening scene of My Week with Marilyn. (© The Weinstein Company)

has no such fine shadings. This is a dumb, affable showgirl and nothing more, and Miss Monroe goes through the motions with mirth, childish innocence, squeals of pleasure, pouts of arrogance, eyes big as golf balls, and many a delighted toss of her rounded surfaces.

Likewise, *New York World-Telegram and Sun* noted, 'She is captivatingly kittenish in her infectious mirth. Her love scenes are played with a girlish game. She romps through slapstick and turns solemn moments into part of her fun.'
As casting began for *My Week with Marilyn*, some early reports mentioned actresses Scarlett Johansson, Amy Adams and Kate Hudson as possible candidates for the lead role, while some have insisted that Michelle Williams had always been the first choice. Williams had small film and TV appearances as a teenager, before her role in the popular television series *Dawson's Creek* (Kevin Williamson, the WB, 1998–2003) launched her career, landing her memorable turns in *Dick* (Andrew Fleming, 1999), *The Station Agent* (Thomas McCarthy, 2003), *Brokeback Mountain* (Ang Lee, 2005), *Wendy and Lucy* (Kelly Reichardt, 2008), Derek Cianfrance's *Blue Valentine* and Reichardt's *Meek's Cutoff* (both 2010), among other award-winning performances. As to be expected, Curtis praised Williams for her decision to tackle such a formidable role, saying that she 'had the courage of a lion taking on this part'. Williams admitted that since there are so many interpretations of Marilyn, she had to go with her own.
Williams embodies Marilyn from the opening scene, as Colin watches her on-screen, singing the 'Heat Wave' number from *There's No Business like Show Business* (Walter Lang, 1954). Admittedly, this is an ambitious move by the film-makers to begin with Williams singing one of Marilyn's best-known numbers, as audiences will already start to compare Williams with Marilyn – evaluating her voice, her look, her charisma. Williams arguably best exhibits Marilyn's charm when she executes the dance from *The Prince and the Showgirl* while alone in the drawing room. Marilyn's vulnerability perhaps comes

Fig. 5: Marilyn Monroe (Michelle Williams) with some of her adoring fans in My Week With Marilyn (© The Weinstein Company)

through most vividly when Colin enters Marilyn's dressing room when she is late for the read through. Sans make-up and in front of her mirror, Williams's reflection captures the nervousness in Marilyn's eyes, even for something as mundane as a pre-rehearsal read through.

Generally fans were pleased to see a biopic that did not dwell on Marilyn as a tragic figure. There were those fans, however, already skeptical of the book *My Week with Marilyn*, since it followed *The Prince, the Showgirl, and Me* by five years, and that earlier book generally has a harsh tone towards its subject. Marilyn scholars and biographers have questioned the authenticity of the books, but if Clark did not pen them in the 1950s, why keep all of his statements bordering on anti-Semitism? And, if Clark were really making most of it up, why not go all the way and claim to actually having had sex with Marilyn, not just a kiss while skinny dipping? Whatever the opinions of Marilyn's fans toward the film, it stands as a notable work, the most important cinematic recreation yet of Marilyn, and will be a key text in the popular imagination of Marilyn. Even if Williams does not quite recreate what it was that made Marilyn so magical, *My Week with Marilyn* may inspire a new generation of Marilyn fans.

None of the previous Marilyn biopics, or films featuring her as major character, had quite the resonance of *My Week with Marilyn*. These include Larry Buchanan's *Goodbye, Norma Jean* (1976) and its sequel, *Goodnight, Sweet Marilyn* (1989); the Italian production *Io & Marilyn* (Leonardo Pieraccioni, 2009); as well as the TV movies *Marilyn: The Untold Story* (Jack Arnold, John Flynn and Lawrence Schiller, 1980), *This Year's Blonde* (John Erman, 1980), *Marilyn and Me* (John Patterson, 1991) – starring professional Marilyn impersonator Susan Griffiths in the titular role – *Norma Jean & Marilyn* (Tim Fywell, 1996), *Marilyn & Bobby: Her Final Affair* (Bradford May, 1993), and the miniseries *Blonde* (Joyce Chopra, CBS, 2001), based on Joyce Carol Oates's book of the same title (published in 2000). Earlier Marilyn performances couldn't compare to Williams's new incarnation, according to Lou Leminik of the *New York Post*:

> Brilliantly playing doomed '50s sex bomb Marilyn Monroe, Michelle Williams gets under the skin of the troubled yet vulnerable icon in a way no one else ever has. Her extraordinary performance in *My Week with Marilyn* makes all of the many performers who have played Monroe previously seem like cheap imitators.

Previous Marilyn portrayals had not drawn the kind of critical notices that Williams received, which were nigh universal in their praise. Mick LaSalle of the *San Francisco Chronicle* stated,

> It takes a lot of courage to play Marilyn Monroe [...] Marilyn was as self-fabricated as Mae West, and to play her is to act like an act. It's a recipe to end up phonier than phony. Yet in *My Week with Marilyn*, Michelle Williams doesn't just survive. Called

Performing Marilyn: Michelle Williams in *My Week with Marilyn*
Zachary Ingle

upon to glow, she glows. Her performance doesn't solve all the riddles of that personality; none could, and it's for the best that Williams doesn't try.

Joe Williams of the *St. Louis Dispatch* labelled her performance

a more three-dimensional Monroe than the love goddess herself. The performance is both an eerie imitation and a touching revelation. Oscar voters who overlooked Williams for her camouflage roles in *Brokeback Mountain*, *Wendy and Lucy*, and *Blue Valentine* should now throw diamonds at her feet.

Roger Ebert also praised Williams's portrayal, clarifying,

The movie seems to be a fairly accurate re-creation of the making of a film at Pinewood Studios at that time. It hardly matters. What happens during the famous week hardly matters. What matters is the performance by Michelle Williams.

To *The Philadelphia Inquirer*'s Carrie Rickey, 'Williams never defaults to mimicry […] Her performance is not an achievement of the makeup department but an imaginative interpretation of an unstable element.' In a similar vein Bob Mondello, chief critic for National Public Radio, states: 'Williams, though she doesn't really resemble Monroe in either voice or visage, is pretty splendid at conjuring her. It's not an impersonation, exactly; for much of the picture, she seems more mousy Norma Jean Mortenson than sexy starlet.'

While most reviewers gushed over Williams's performance, some were less than enthusiastic about the film, as in this typical review, courtesy of *Arizona Republic*'s Bill Goodykoontz: 'If *My Week with Marilyn* ultimately seems like a slight film, a barely disguised awards vehicle for Williams, that's probably because it is. But her performance is so engaging and complete, it's worth all the other shortcomings.' Concerning the film itself, *Chicago Reader*'s J. R. Jones commented, 'There's nothing new here about Marilyn that we haven't been told a thousand times already: she was sexy, she was troubled; she was warm, she was selfish; she took pills, she lit up the screen.' Or this one, from a generally positive review from *Salon.com*'s Andrew O'Hehir: '*The King's Speech* has the subtlety of Chekhov in comparison.' Other derisive appellations appended to the film were 'lugubrious', 'fluffy entertainment' and 'intentionally minor', but any dissenting voices criticizing Williams were noticeably absent.

Indeed, Williams's performance in *My Week with Marilyn* surpassed previous incarnations of the icon. Various critical and awards bodies lauded Williams's performance, as she won a Golden Globe (Best Actress in a Motion Picture Musical or Comedy) and an Independent Spirit Award for Best Actress, as well as similar kudos from the film critics of Toronto, Washington DC, Las Vegas, Florida, Utah, Oklahoma, Detroit, Dallas-Ft.

Fig. 6: Michelle Williams was awarded the Golden Globe for her performance as Marilyn Monroe in My Week with Marilyn. (© The Weinstein Company)

Worth, Chicago, Central Ohio and Boston, and was also nominated for the Best Actress Oscar. While Marilyn appears as a minor character in several recent productions including the Canadian-US miniseries *The Kennedys* (Jon Cassar, History Television), released in 2011 – in which Charlotte Sullivan does not make a convincing Marilyn – Andrew Dominik's forthcoming *Blonde*, based on the eponymous Joyce Carol Oates book (as is the 2001 CBS miniseries *Blonde*) and starring Jessica Chastain, is slated for release in 2016. *My Week with Marilyn* may be the most popular and critically acclaimed Marilyn performance yet, and while Williams's place in Marilyn lore is now assured, Marilyn fans also acknowledge that there has been, and always will be, only one Marilyn Monroe. ●

GO FURTHER

Books
My Week with Marilyn
Colin Clark
(New York: Weinstein Books, 2011)
[This edition combines both *My Week with Marilyn* and *The Prince, the Showgirl, and Me*.]

Blonde: A Novel
Joyce Carol Oates
(New York: Echo Press, 2000)

The Marilyn Encyclopedia
Adam Victor
(Woodstock, NY: Overlook Press, 1999), pp. 239-240 (reviews of *The Prince and the Showgirl*)

Online
Articles
'*My Week With Marilyn*'
Roger Ebert
RogerEbert.com. 21 November 2011,
http://www.rogerebert.com/reviews/my-week-with-marilyn-2011

'*My Week With Marilyn*: 4 Stars'
Bill Goodykoontz
AZcentral.com. 22 November 2011,

Performing Marilyn: Michelle Williams in *My Week with Marilyn*
Zachary Ingle

http://www.azcentral.com/thingstodo/movies/articles/2011/11/18/20111118my-week-marilyn-movie-review-goodykoontz.html

'Michelle Williams: My Week with Michelle'
Adam Green
Vogue.com, Portraits and cover photo by Annie Liebovitz. 13 September 2011, http://www.vogue.com/magazine/article/michelle-williams-my-week-with-michelle/#1.

'*My Week With Marilyn*'
J.R. Jones
ChicagoReader.com,
http://www.chicagoreader.com/chicago/my-week-with-marilyn/Film?oid=4800506

'Mystery Surrounds *My Week with Marilyn*'
Amy Kaufman
Los Angeles Times.com. 11 December 2011, http://articles.latimes.com/2011/dec/10/entertainment/la-etmarilyn-accuracy-20111210.

'*My Week With Marilyn* Review: Still Aglow'
Mick LaSalle
Sfgate.com. 23 November 2011,
http://www.sfgate.com/movies/article/My-Week-With-Marilyn-review-Still-aglow-2290442.php

'A Sweet and Fated *Marilyn*'
Lou Lumenick
New York Post.com. 23 November 2011,
http://nypost.com/2011/11/23/a-sweet-fated-marilyn/

'A Prince and A Showgirl, On Location and At Odds'
Bob Mondello
NPR.org. 22 November 2011,
http://www.npr.org/2011/11/22/142504811/a-prince-and-a-showgirl-on-location-and-at-odds

'*My Week With Marilyn*: Michelle Williams' Dazzling Oscar Bid'
Andrew O'Hehir
Salon.com. 22 November 2011,
http://www.salon.com/2011/11/23/my_week_with_marilyn_michelle_williams_dazzling_oscar_bid/

'The Clash of Bombshell and Brit'
Carrie Rickey
Philly.com. 23 November 2011,
http://www.philly.com/philly/columnists/carrie_rickey/20111123_The_clash_of_bomb-shell_and_Brit.html

Websites
Susan Griffiths Performing as Marilyn Monroe: http://www.susangriffiths.com/

Films/Television
Marilyn biopics
Blonde, Andrew Dominik, dir. (United States: New Regency Pictures/Plan B Entertainment, forthcoming, 2016).

My Week with Marilyn, Simon Curtis, dir. (United States: The Weinstein Company/ Great Britain: BBC Films, Trademark Films, 2011).

The Kennedys, Jon Cassar, dir. (Canada: Muse Entertainment Enterprises/United States: Asylum Entertainment, 2011).

Io & Marilyn, Leonardo Pieraccioni, dir. (Italy: Medusa Film/Levante Film, 2009).

The Prince, the Showgirl, and Me, Claire Beavan, dir. (Great Britain: BBC, 2004).

Blonde, Joyce Chopra, dir. (United States: CBS, 2001).

Norma Jean & Marilyn, Tim Fywell, dir. (United States: HBO, 1996).

Marilyn & Bobby: Her Final Affair, Bradford May, dir. (United States: Barry Weitz Films/ The Auerbach Company, 1993).

Marilyn and Me, John Patterson, dir. (United States: Poochie Productions/Samuels Film Company, 1991).

Marilyn: The Untold Story, Jack Arnold, John Flynn and Lawrence Schiller, dirs. (United States: Schiller Productions, Inc., 1980).

This Year's Blonde, John Erman, dir. (United States: Warner Bros. Television, 1980).

Performing Marilyn: Michelle Williams in *My Week with Marilyn*
Zachary Ingle

Goodbye, Norma Jean, Larry Buchanan, dir. (Austamerican Productions, 1976).

Michelle Williams filmography
Blue Valentine, Derek Cianfrance, dir. (United States: Incentive Filmed Entertainment/ Silverwood Films/Hunting Lane Films, 2010).

Meek's Cutoff, Kelly Reichardt, dir (United States: Evenstar Films/Film Science/Glass Eye Pix, 2010).

Wendy and Lucy, Kelly Reichardt, dir. (United States: Field Guide Films, 2008).

Brokeback Mountain, Ang Lee, dir. (United States: Focus Features, 2005).

The Station Agent, Thomas McCarthy, dir. (United States: SenArt Films/Next Wednesday Productions, 2003).

Dawson's Creek, Kevin Williamson, creator (United States: Outerbank Entertainment/ Columbia TriStar Television, 1998–2003).

Dick, Andrew Fleming, dir. (United States: Canal+ D.A./Pacific Western, 1999).

Other films referenced
Thor, Kenneth Branagh, dir. (United States: Paramount Pictures/Marvel Entertainment, 2011).

The King's Speech, Tom Hooper, dir. (United States: The Weinstein Company, 2010/ Great Britain: UK Film Council).

Pulp Fiction, Quentin Tarantino, dir. (United States: Miramax/A Band Apart, 1994).

The Prince and the Showgirl, Laurence Olivier, dir. (United States: Warner Bros., 1957).

'I KNEW I BELONGED TO THE PUBLIC AND TO THE WORLD, NOT BECAUSE I WAS TALENTED OR EVEN BEAUTIFUL, BUT BECAUSE I HAD NEVER BELONGED TO ANYTHING OR ANYONE ELSE.'

MARILYN MONROE

Fan Appreciation no.4
Tara Hanks, author of *The MMM Girl*

*Figure 1: Marilyn Monroe fan-
author Tara Hanks posing
with her book, The MMM Girl
(©Tara Hanks).*

Authors' statement:

While writing my novel *The MMM Girl*, I was able to learn about other fans' perspectives on aspects of Marilyn's life story. I was able to get a more detailed picture of specific events through rare photos and articles shared by fans. I also received a great deal of support for my book, which is invaluable to any writer. *The MMM Girl* was promoted widely within the fan community. On a personal level, I've made many lasting friendships with Marilyn fans, particularly other writers and artists.

Since the publication of *The MM Girl* in late 2007, I have remained active within the fandom. I now maintain the *Everlasting-Star Updates* blog (www.blog.everlasting-star.net) and am always surprised by how widely Marilyn's influence has spread. I review books about her on my personal website (www.tarahanks.com), and contribute articles about a variety of topics on http://www.immortalmarilyn.com/.

'The Camera Loved Her':
Excerpt from *The MMM Girl: Marilyn Monroe, by Herself...*
by Tara Hanks (UKA Press, 2007)

Tobey Beach, 1949
White sand stretched for miles, overlooking the ocean. Families played together, paddling and building sandcastles. But Andre headed past the bay to a deserted area. He set up near the tide, while I changed into a white bathing suit.

Down on the beach, I held up the parasol, opened it wide, and twirled it in the air. Then I put it at my side and danced around it. Andre took it away and I ran into the sea, swimming just far enough to soak my hair and skin.

'Your hair... it's different,' he said. 'Where do you get it done?'

'It's called strawberry blonde,' I answered. 'Johnny likes it platinum. But this is more natural, isn't it?'

The sun had dried me a little. We moved back from the shore and I posed again, running, jumping or just standing still.

'Where are you living?' he asked. 'Is your mother with you?'

I looked away, remembering the time I visited her in Oregon and how she'd begged me to let her come home. That night, I'd gone to bed with Andre, though I was still married to Jim.

'I often think of how she upset you,' Andre said, rolling a cigarette. His brown hair was receding, but his voice was as husky and seductive as ever.

'Mother's in California,' I told him. 'She just got married again.'

Aunt Grace had told me about it. Mother's new husband was an electri-

Fan Appreciation no.4
Tara Hanks, author of *The MMM Girl*

cian who worked at the state hospital where she'd recently been a patient.

'My poor darling,' Andre said, softly. 'You must be so afraid that one day you'll end up crazy like her.'

I pulled on a white toweling robe and dropped to the sand. He started another roll of film. I knelt with my eyes closed and put my hands together in prayer, and Andre snapped around me.

'Think of anything,' he said. 'You might be imagining what real love is like.'

Daylight was fading fast. I picked up the scarf and held it against my body, dancing again.

On the drive back to Manhattan, I sipped from a flask of coffee.

'This affair of yours, with that old man. Is it serious? I can't believe he satisfies you.' Andre reached out to touch my leg, but I dodged him quickly. 'I never saw you as a gold digger, but Hollywood's changed you.'

'He says I make him happy.' I smiled as I thought of Johnny, who called every night at eight. 'Isn't that what really matters, Andre?'

He braked sharply and the car screamed to a halt. City drivers tooted their horns. He forced a kiss on me, and I backed away.

'Like you said, I've changed. But we can be friends, can't we?'

Andre dropped me off by the hotel. Next morning he left a note at reception, asking me to pose nude. I hadn't told him about the calendar job, and I never sent a reply.

Laurel Canyon, 1953
The midday sun burned over Laurel Canyon, and I took off my dark glasses and reached into my purse for more lipstick.

'We'll shoot over here by this rock.' Milton Greene smiled gently. 'Just relax, don't pose.'

Look magazine had sent him from New York to do a feature.

I sat cross-legged on the dusty ground. Behind me, the granite was white-hot, and it blended with my linen blouse and pants.

'It's so quiet,' I said. 'Do you like living in the country?'

'Oh, yes. Amy loves Connecticut, and she's always entertaining. It's like Manhattan, but without the pressure.'

'Must be good for your baby, too – healthier, I mean.' Milton's assistant poured champagne, and I raised my glass. 'This is my best session in a long time,' I said. 'Most guys just tell me to look sexy.'

'Not what I'm after,' Milt said. 'But don't worry – I won't turn you into a frump, either.'

'Why don't we walk,' his assistant said. 'There's a farm down the hill, and we could take more pictures.'

He led the way and I followed with Milt, brushing against the sage and eucalyptus that grew wild along the track.

Scrambling across a field, I took Milt's arm.

'How old are you?' I asked, reaching up to touch his cheek.

'Thirty,' he said, grinning.

'And you look like a boy of twenty!'

'Well, you're just a girl,' he said. 'Something's missing, though. You have everything you could want, but you're not satisfied.'

We sat down by a haystack. My hair was mussed, and my lipstick had worn off again, so I put on my sunglasses and shared a cigarette with Milton.

'If I got the chance to produce a movie, I'd let you play anything you choose. Marilyn, I mean it – you're not a flash in the pan.'

'Maybe we should go into business,' I said, watching him closely as he stood up and stubbed the cigarette underfoot.

We went back to the car, and planned our afternoon. After a change of clothes, I led the others into woodland and sat under an oak tree. Later we did some studio shots, for which I was naked under a long cashmere sweater.

New York, 1958

'Gee, I don't look like me at all.'

I adjusted my wig, and Arthur held up a mirror.

'You really could be Clara Bow,' he said.

'Well, my mother had red hair like hers.'

The make-up girl re-applied my lipstick, shaping my mouth into a cupid's bow.

'Thanks,' I said. Pink and red balloons and streamers hung from the ceiling, and a white curtain was draped over the set.

'Are you sure you're ready for this?' asked Richie Avedon, the photographer. 'It'll take a little while.'

All day I'd been posing, first as Marlene Dietrich, then Theda Bara and Lillian Russell. Now I was Clara Bow.

'Sure, this is fun.' I laughed. 'I'm not tired at all.'

Richie put a bottle of champagne in the bucket, and I pulled my fringed red dress into place.

In the first shots I danced the Charleston, just as Grace had once taught me. I bent down, picked up a red feather, turned my head to Richie, and pouted.

'Here, have some champagne,' he said, and his assistant brought a glass. I opened the bottle, the cork flew out, and I jumped back.

Fan Appreciation no.4
Tara Hanks, author of *The MMM Girl*

'This is just like my last picture,' I said, 'only much more fun.'

Arthur and Richie were both New Yorkers, and with their dark hair and glasses, they looked similar. But Richie enjoyed being around people a lot more than Arthur did.

'For stills, you're using heavy lights,' I commented.

'I wanted to get the feel of a movie set. If you like, I'll take you through to the darkroom. The prints should be done now.'

Arthur followed, and together we sorted through contact sheets. A few had me riding a bicycle, in a corset and a large flowered hat.

'Her style really flatters a woman's curves,' I said, holding one print up. 'Mae West used to dress like this, too.'

'Yes,' Richie said, 'though I'm not sure you're fleshy enough for Diamond Lil.'

'That makes a change! My first agent said I was too curvy for fashion.'

'Ah, you're a natural.' Arthur studied the prints. He was writing an article about me, to go with the pictures.

We skimmed through sheets of poses, some with me in Egyptian costume, prowling across a tigerskin rug. In another sequence, I'd recreated scenes from *Blue Angel* in suspenders and a top hat.

'I feel so close to these actresses,' I said. 'When I was growing up, I'd see them on the screen and wish I could be like them.'

'And now you're playing them.' Arthur took a leisurely pull on his pipe.

'Let's go and do more,' I told Richie. 'If you don't mind, I could stay here all night. Let's do Harlow next.'

Back in the dressing room, I took off my red dress and wig. The girl applied a white foundation, and I put on another hairpiece. It was real platinum white-blonde, lighter than my own hair color.

'Jean always wore white.' I told Arthur, sifting through pictures. 'Look at this. Even her furnishings were white – just like the house I lived in with Mother and Grace.'

After a net curtain had been added to the backdrop, I leaned back against a couch. Richie brought in a dog to sit at my feet, and I stroked him. A few seconds later, I suddenly sank back on the couch, lost in a kind of sadness.

'Darling, you're exhausted.' Arthur came over and knelt beside me. 'Come on, I'll drive you home.'

'You're right, I know. But tonight I felt like a real actress, and maybe Jean was, too. Nobody saw that, until she was gone.'

Arthur helped me up and I went over to Richie, who hugged me. I kissed him, and returned to the dressing room.

Santa Monica, 1962

I was in my yellow bikini. Agnes was brushing my hair. The sky was overcast, and a cool wind blew across Santa Monica Beach. Across the pier, Peter's house was half-visible in the mist.

'Want some more?' Whitey handed me a glass of champagne. I took a quick sip, rummaged through my make-up bag, found a tub of Vaseline and smeared some over my dry skin.

George, the photographer, came over. His cameras were set up again, and he wanted more pictures before the sun went down.

'This is the real me,' I said.

I pointed at my freckles, and the surgical scar.

'Do you know this place?' George asked.

'Yes, my mother used to bring me here.' I glanced up at the palms, and the hills. On Sundays Mother had taken me to the fair.

'Go into the water,' George said.

'I'm not much of a swimmer,' I protested, but he smiled.

I ran along the sand, feeling it damp between my toes.

'You look like a little girl,' George called encouragingly.

'Norma Jeane!' I yelled back. 'That's my real name.'

I ran out further, and waves crashed past. I bent slightly, my arms spread wide. Seagulls flew by, crying their way to Catalina Island.

'Come back!' George hollered.

I waded out of the water. George passed me an orange scarf and I wound it round my neck, took a deep breath, and held in my stomach.

'Are you cold?' George asked.

'Fine, thanks – let's get moving.' I took off the scarf and leaned forward, digging my hands into the sand. Stretching further, I remembered posing for countless photographers on beaches like this.

'Here, catch.'

George threw a towel and I wrapped myself in it.

I asked for champagne and drank slowly while George took pictures.

'Hope these come out.' He put another roll into the camera.

'Send the others to *Cosmopolitan*,' I said, 'the ones we took at your friend's house. But we should keep these to ourselves. One day I'm going to write my life story – the same one I started years ago, but never finished.'

'And you'd like to use these pictures?'

'Yes.' I sat down, my legs covered by the towel. 'This is where it began, in Santa Monica. And you can help, just by showing me as I really am.'

Fan Appreciation no.4
Tara Hanks, author of *The MMM Girl*

A crowd was watching. I waved. One old lady on a lounger, her face hidden by sunglasses, had been here since we arrived, flipping through magazines.

'Wonder who she is?' I said. 'When my mother got sick, there was an old lady who let me stay with her… She was very kind.'

'Older people love you.' George smiled. 'And children.'

'And they're the ones who never hurt us.'

I lay on my side, peeking at George through my fingers. He laughed. After a few more shots, I walked back out towards the sea. The wind was growing colder, and hair blew across my face.

I closed my eyes and hugged myself. When I looked around and saw George again, I broke into a smile. The light was fading. I sat down on the sand, clasped my hands and blew a kiss.

'For you, George,' I said.

He put down his camera, and I got dressed. Rudy drove me home. I told Mrs Murray to leave, and went straight to bed. My prescriptions were by the door. ●

GO FURTHER

Books
Marilyn
Andre de Dienes, Steve Crist and Shirley T. Ellis de Dienes (eds)
(Taschen Press, 2007)

The MMM Girl: Marilyn Monroe, by Herself…
Tara Hanks
(Great Britain: UKA Press, 2007; 2nd ed., Create Space Independent Publishing, 2015)
[Winner of the UKA Press Opening Pages Competition.]

Marilyn: Her Life in Her Own Words:
Marilyn Monroe's Revealing Last Words and Photographs
George Barris
(New York: Citadel Press, repr. edn, 2001)

Milton's Marilyn: The Photographs of Milton H. Greene
Milton H. Greene
(New York: Schirmer Books, 1995)

Marilyn, Mon Amour: The Private Album of Andre de Dienes, Her Preferred Photographer
Andre de Dienes
(New York: St. Martin's, 1985)

Magazines
'Marilyn Monroe in a Remarkable Re-creation of Fabled Enchantresses'
Photos by Richard Avedon
Life. 22 December 1958: 138-146.

'My Wife, Marilyn'
Arthur Miller
Life. 22 December 1958: 146-147.

Online
Tara Hanks: http://tarahanks.com/
Everlasting-Star Updates by Tara Hanks: http://www.everlasting-star.net
Review of *The MMM Girl* by Fraser Penney at *Immortal Marilyn*: http://www.immortalmarilyn.com/BOTMMmmGirl.html
Jeremy Richey's Interview with Tara Hanks at *Moon in the Gutter*: http://mooninthegutter.blogspot.com/2010/06/moon-in-gutter-q-with-author-tara-hanks.html
'Marilyn's Heroes', a series of articles by Tara Hanks: http://www.immortalmarilyn.com/MarilynsHeroes.html

Chapter
6

The 50th Anniversary of Marilyn Monroe's Death

Scott Fortner

→ The morning of 6 August 1962, the headline of the *New York Daily News* read, 'Marilyn Dead.' The world was in shock. The sex goddess of the silver screen was gone. Hadn't she sung 'Happy Birthday' to President Kennedy barely three months earlier? Alas, the little girl from the orphanage had succumbed, and 50 years later, there is still heated debate surrounding the cause of her death: was it suicide, murder, accidental overdose?

Fig. 1: Front page of The Daily News announcing Marilyn Monroe's death, Monday, 6 August 1962.

Fig. 2: Cover of the programme for the 50th Anniversary Memorial Service for Marilyn Monroe (© Scott Fortner)

Her funeral on 8 August was arranged by Joe DiMaggio, with the help of Marilyn's half-sister Berniece Baker Miracle, and Inez Melson, Marilyn's business manager. Only Marilyn's closest friends and family members were invited. Hollywood's elite were turned away at the entrance to Westwood Memorial Park where the service was held, and where Marilyn was entombed for eternity.

Joe DiMaggio had roses delivered to Marilyn's crypts on a weekly basis for decades after her passing. Amazingly, there were no other formal memorials or services for the most famous blonde of all time. On 5 August 1982, four of Marilyn's devoted fans – Anthony Cordova, Greg Schreiner, Catherine Seeger and Teresa Seeger – met at her crypt for the first time, and the Marilyn Remembered Fan Club was formed, whose mission is to preserve the memory of Marilyn Monroe with dignity and grace. Of the four fans that met in 1982, Greg Schreiner is still active with Marilyn Remembered, and he has organized an annual memorial service for Marilyn each year for nearly thirty years. The memorials have all been held at Westwood Memorial Park, and have featured guests and speakers directly related to/ associated with Marilyn: film co-stars, hairstylists, stand-ins, and many others who knew Marilyn personally and shared their stories.

The fifth of August, 2012 marked the 50th anniversary of Marilyn's passing, and as such, was the largest memorial service for Marilyn Monroe held to date. The memorial service committee consisted of eight devoted fans: Rick Carl, Amy Condit, Jackie Craig, Michelle Justice, Leah Peterson, Greg Schreiner, Amy Ulrich and myself.

Planning for the 2012 memorial service began almost immediately after the 2011 memorial service commenced. The buildup for the 50th anniversary memorial was already beginning, and 2012 was to be Marilyn's year.

As in recent years, Marilyn Remembered reached out to fans and offered the opportunity to sponsor the event. Nearly 150 Marilyn Monroe fans and several fan clubs from around the world donated funds to help offset the costs of the memorial service. Two corporate sponsors also helped fund the event: the Hollywood Museum and Heritage Auctions. With the money collected from the sponsors, the committee made arrangements for a reception to follow the service, flowers for the chapel, and an awning and chairs for overflow guests seated outside of the chapel. Guests seated outside were still able to watch the service thanks to a videographer who was filming the service and also broadcasting it on a large-screen television situated outside under the awning. The committee also designed a glossy colour memorial service programme, which was free to every guest attending the service [Editor's note: see images of the cover and interior

The 50th Anniversary of Marilyn Monroe's Death
Scott Fortner

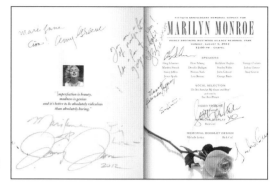

of the memorial service programme, which are enclosed herewith].

For the first time ever, Amy Greene – photographer Milton Greene's wife – made an appearance at a memorial service, and also for the first time, Marilyn Monroe's half-sister, Berniece Baker Miracle and Berniece's daughter, Mona Rae Miracle, provided a message to be read to Marilyn's fans.

Other speakers at the 2012 Marilyn Monroe Memorial Service who also offered rich insight into the legend include the following:

> Greg Schreiner, President, Marilyn Remembered Fan Club
> Manfred Strunk, President, Some Like It Hot International Marilyn Monroe Fan Club (Germany)
> Nancy Jeffries, Marilyn's foster sister
> James Spada, Author, *Monroe: Her Life in Pictures* (1982)
> Peter Schnug, Film Historian and fan
> Donelle Dadigan, Fan and President, The Hollywood Museum
> Lois Banner, Ph.D., Historian and Author, *Marilyn: The Passion and The Paradox* (2012) and *MM-Personal* (2010); Professor Emerita, University of Southern California
> Kathleen Hughes, Actress, *It Came from Outer Space* (Jack Arnold, 1953); and wife of producer Stanley Rubin
> Stanley Rubin, Producer, *River of No Return* (Otto Preminger, 1954)
> John Gilmore, Actor and Author of *Inside Marilyn Monroe: A Memoir* (2007)
> George Barris, Photographer
> George Chakiris, Dancer and Academy Award-winning Actor, *West Side Story* (Robert Wise and Jerome Robbins, 1961)
> Joshua Greene, Photographer and son of photographer Milton Greene
> Amy Greene, wife of photographer Milton Greene

Fig. 3/4: Interior pages and contents of the programme for the 50th Anniversary Memorial Service for Marilyn Monroe (courtesy Marijane Gray).

Select readings were also delivered from the Sam Shaw Family, and Douglas Kirkland.

The vocal selection for the service, 'Do Not Stand at My Grave and Weep', written by Greg Schreiner, was performed by Emmy Award-winning singer Sue Ann Pinner. Original artwork, created by Rick Carl and flanked by many sprays of flowers, took centre stage in the chapel. The service concluded with a video that I (Scott Fortner) created portraying images of Marilyn Monroe, coupled with a recording of the actual eulogy delivered by Lee Strasberg at Marilyn's funeral.

Hundreds of Marilyn Monroe fans from around the world converged on Los Ange-

Fig. 5: Jackie Craig, Immortal Marilyn's LA Representative, at the 52nd Anniversary Memorial of Marilyn Monroe's passing. Jackie Craig, a leading figure in the MM fandom community—in both Immortal Marilyn and Marilyn Remembered—is holding the 2014 Memorial Program, which she helped distribute. (© Jackie Craig)

les in August 2012 to commemorate Marilyn's life during a memorable week entirely devoted to festivities held in her honour, including an exhibit at the Hollywood Museum consisting of the collections of Scott Fortner and Greg Schreiner; a tour of Twentieth Century Fox; a pool party at the Orchid Suites; a tour of Marilyn's homes and haunts; Marilyn Monroe film screenings, book signings and other Marilyn-themed activities.

More information about Marilyn Remembered, the longest running Marilyn Monroe fan club in existence today, is available at www.MarilynRemembered.org. Membership is free, and is open to Marilyn Monroe fans around the world.

Marilyn always said, 'hold a good thought for me.' With the success of the 2012 Marilyn Monroe Memorial Service, and all of the memorials before and those yet to come, we hope we have done just that. ●

GO FURTHER

Books

Marilyn: The Passion and the Paradox
Lois Banner
(New York: Bloomsbury, 2012)

MM-Personal: From the Private Archive of Marilyn Monroe
Lois Banner
(New York: Abrams, 2010)

Inside Marilyn Monroe: A Memoir
John Gilmore
(Ferine Books, 2007)

Marilyn: Her Life in Her Own Words: Marilyn Monroe's Revealing Last Words and Photographs
George Barris
(Secaucus, NJ: Carol Pub. Group, 1995)

Milton's Marilyn: The Photographs of Milton H. Greene
Milton H. Greene and James Kotsilibas-Davis
(New York: Schirmer Books, 1995)

The 50th Anniversary of Marilyn Monroe's Death
Scott Fortner

My Sister Marilyn: A Memoir of Marilyn Monroe
Berniece Baker Miracle and Mona Rae Miracle
(Chapel Hill, NC: Algonquin Books of Chapel Hill, 1994)

Monroe: Her Life in Pictures
James Spada, with George Zeno
(New York: Doubleday, 1982)

Chapters
'Kathleen Hughes: Western Scream Queen'
In Michael Fitzgerald and Boyd Magers (eds). *Ladies of the Western: Interviews with Fifty-One More Actresses from the Silent Era to the Television Westerns of the 1950s and 1960s*
(Jefferson, North Carolina: McFarland, 2006), pp. 88–92.

'The Marilyn Monroe Half-Centennial Memorial'
In Gary Vitacco-Robles, *Icon: The Life, Times, and Films of Marilyn Monroe, vol. 2: 1956-1962 & Beyond.*
(Albany, Georgia: BearManor Media, November 2014), 665-678.
[NB: This chapter was published in November 2014 when *Fan Phenomena: Marilyn Monroe* was in press with Scott Fortner's text, about the 50th MM memorial, commissioned by Marcelline Block in August 2012]

Online
Articles
'Goodbye Norma Jeane: The 51st Anniversary of Marilyn Monroe's Death'
Ariana Lange
Buzzfeed. 6 August 2013, http://www.buzzfeed.com/arianelange/the-51st-anniversary-of-marilyn-monroes-death.

'Marilyn Monroe: 50th Anniversary of Her Death Commemorated at Her Westwood Cemetery' Bill Raden
LA Weekly. 6 August 2012, http://www.laweekly.com/publicspectacle/2012/08/06/marilyn-monroe-50th-anniversary-of-her-death-commemorated-at-her-westwood-cemetery.

Websites
August 5, 2012, Marilyn Monroe's 50th Anniversary Memorial:
http://www.immortalmarilyn.com/2012Aug5.html

Heritage Auctions: http://www.ha.com
The Hollywood Museum 2012 Marilyn Monroe Memorial Service: http://thehollywoodmuseum.com/marilynmemorialservice2012/
Immortal Marilyn's 50th Anniversary Memorial Homepage: http://www.immortalmarilyn.com/2012MemorialPage.html
Lee Strasberg's Eulogy for Marilyn Monroe (full text): http://blog.everlasting-star.net/2010/08/anniversaries/eulogy-for-marilyn/
'Marilyn Monroe and Me', an online photo exhibition of fans visiting Marilyn Monroe's crypt, curated by Scott Fortner: http://themarilynmonroecollection.com/marilyn-monroe-and-me/
Marilyn Monroe Year-Round Exhibit at the Hollywood Museum, featuring items from Scott Fortner's Collection: http://thehollywoodmuseum.com/exhibit/marilyn-year-round-exhibit-at-the-hollywood-museum/
Marilyn Remembered, 'Preserving the Memory of Marilyn Monroe with Dignity and Grace since 1982': www.MarilynRemembered.org
Some Like It Hot International Marilyn Monroe Fan Club (Germany): http://www.marilyn-monroe-fanclub.de/index.htm
Greg Schreiner's The Marilyn Monroe Site: http://www.themarilynmonroesite.com
Peter Schnug's speech at the 50th Anniversary Memorial of Marilyn Monroe (video): https://www.youtube.com/watch?v=70nWss-8VEU
Sue Ann Pinner and Greg Schreiner performing 'Do Not Stand at My Grave and Weep': https://www.youtube.com/watch?v=QbYhKYX-gXl

Films

Stanley Rubin: A Work in Progress, Kellett Tighe, dir. (Knock Knock Entertainment/Brilliant Way Productions, 2008).

West Side Story, Robert Wise and Jerome Robbins, dirs. (United States: The Mirisch Corporation/Seven Arts Productions, 1961).

River of No Return, Otto Preminger, dir. (United States: Twentieth Century Fox, 1954).

Fan Appreciation no.5
Melinda Mason, the 'Marilyn Geek'

*Fig. 1: Melinda Mason at
Marilyn Monroe's crypt,
on the 50th anniversary of
Monroe's death, August 2012
(© Melinda Mason).*

Fig. 2: Poster advertising the
exhibition of Melinda Mason's
collection of Marilyn Monroe
items and memorabilia at the
Wellington County Museum
and Archives (Canada),
September 2014-January
2015. (© Wellington County
Museum and Archives)

Interview by Marcelline Block

When I was a teenager, I was a big fan of Madonna. The
'Material Girl' video had just come out where Madonna
was imitating Marilyn's performance of 'Diamonds are a
Girl's Best Friend' [from *Gentlemen Prefer Blondes* (Howard Hawks, 1953)]. I saw a news programme where they did
a comparison between the two and I thought Marilyn was
the most beautiful woman I had ever seen. I picked up a
biography about her and was hooked.

I started a Marilyn Monroe website in August 2000
and was lucky enough to grab the domain name marilyn-
monroe.ca. It is one of the longest running Marilyn sites
on the Internet and therefore is also one of the most popular. I have had over a million visitors. I get e-mails every
day from fans all over the world. I spend a considerable
amount of my free time responding to questions from
new fans and collectors. I think of myself as a Marilyn ambassador since many new fans get their very first information about Marilyn from my website.

I have had the opportunity to travel to Hollywood several times to commemorate the anniversary of her death with other fans. It is amazing to
meet fans from all over the world. In 2007, I shared a room with fans from
Belgium and Australia who I had only met online previously. It was one of
the best experiences of my life. For the 50th anniversary of Marilyn's death
in 2012, I arranged transportation for 40 fans to go from Hollywood to the
Del Coronado Hotel in San Diego. This is the location where *Some Like It
Hot* [Billy Wilder, 1959] was filmed. It was truly incredible to stand on the
same beach where Marilyn stood over fifty years ago. I loved being able to
give this experience to other fans. Marilyn has given me a passion in my life
and a real feeling of purpose. It is always a thrill when I meet someone and
they tell me that they became a Marilyn fan because of my website. I enjoy
being considered a Marilyn expert. I have been acknowledged in several
Marilyn books and have appeared on television as well. ●

(Answers have been edited and condensed)

Biographical note
Melinda Mason was born, raised and still lives in Fergus, Ontario, Canada.
She has been a Marilyn Monroe fan and collector for 25 years. She is the

Fan Appreciation no.5
Melinda Mason, the 'Marilyn Geek'

webmaster of www.marilynmonroe.ca, one of the longest running Marilyn websites on the Internet. Melinda had the wedding of her dreams in 2010 in Las Vegas on Marilyn's birthday, 1 June. Two of the world's most famous Marilyn Monroe impersonators, Suzie Kennedy from the UK and Susan Griffiths from LA, were her bridesmaids. Her collection of Marilyn items and memorabilia was exhibited at the Wellington County Museum from September 2014 to January 2015.

GO FURTHER

Online
Websites
Melinda Mason's website, Marilyn Geek (formerly Marilyn and the Camera): www.marilynmonroe.ca
Best Episodes of Melinda Mason's 'My Marilyn Podcast' from 2005–10: http://mymarilyn.libsyn.com/page
Susan Griffiths Performing as Marilyn Monroe: www.susangriffiths.com/
Suzie Kennedy as Marilyn Monroe: http://topmarilynmonroelookalike.co.uk/
'Marilyn Quote UnQuote', Immortal Marilyn (devoted to proving the authenticity of Marilyn Monroe quotations and debunking the proliferation of false quotations attributed to her): http://www.immortalmarilyn.com/QuoteUnQuote.html

Exhibit
The Collection of Melinda Mason, Wellington County Museum and Archives, 12 September 2014-11 January 2015, http://www.wellington.ca/en/discover/wellingtoncountycollectsmelindamason.asp

Films
Some Like It Hot, Billy Wilder, dir. (United States: Ashton Productions/ The Mirisch Corporation, 1959).

Songs
'Diamonds Are a Girl's Best Friend' (Jule Styne and Leo Robin, 1949), sung by Marilyn Monroe in *Gentlemen Prefer Blondes* (Howard Hawks, 1953).

'AND I WANT TO SAY THAT THE PEOPLE – IF I AM A STAR – THEY MADE ME A STAR – NO STUDIO, NO PERSON, BUT THE PEOPLE DID.'

MARILYN MONROE

Fan Appreciation no.6
Marijane Gray

*Fig. 1: Marilyn Monroe fan
Marijane Gray on Santa
Monica Beach where
Marilyn's last photo shoot
was held (© Marijane Gray)*

Interview by Marcelline Block

The most meaningful aspects of being part of the Marilyn Monroe fandom community: First and foremost are the wonderful friends I have made in the Marilyn fan community. There are people that I have gotten to know far beyond our mutual fascination with Marilyn and with whom I have made deep and genuine friendships. I have also been honoured to be able to correspond with the world's leading experts on her, her photographers, biographers and other people who actually knew her. Being part of this community led to one of the best experiences of my life, which was being photographed on the *Seven Year Itch* [Billy Wilder, 1955] subway grate while holding one of her personally owned dresses for publication in a book [NB: *Marilyn & I* by Yury Toroptsov (2011)].

I would have to say, though, there is one particular time that the Marilyn fan community touched my heart like no other. When I attended the 2012 Memorial [NB: the 50th Anniversary Memorial Service for Marilyn Monroe], I finally got to meet my favourite person in the online Marilyn Monroe fan community, my friend Ross McNaughton from Australia. I am so grateful for the time I got to spend with him, especially because when he got home from the trip to LA he was diagnosed with leukemia. Ross had been a Marilyn fan and part of the community for nearly fifty years, and was beloved by people across the globe. One of his friends, Shaney, from the UK, set up a group to raise funds to be able to send him little gifts each week to lift his spirits. Nearly 100 people made sure that he was bombarded with presents while undergoing treatment. Unfortunately, though, it was only eight short months before he passed away. Because Ross was so important to the fan community and had touched so many lives, we wanted to honour him. We held a fundraiser auction in order to have a plaque with his name on it placed at Westwood Cemetery near his beloved Marilyn. The community came together in the most remarkable way. Over fifty different items were generously donated for the auction and many others donated directly. Not only did we raise enough to have his plaque placed there, but also, we were able to make a donation of over four-thousand dollars to the Leukemia Foundation of Queensland in his name.

The way the community came together to honour and pay tribute to one of our members exemplifies how much love we have for each other, how much we mean to one another, and the generosity and kindness of the community as a whole. Marilyn fans are some of the kindest, most generous, and genuine people I've ever had the honour to know. The communities I'm involved in are very tight-knit and close, despite us be-

Fan Appreciation no.6
Marijane Gray

Fig. 2: After the death of Ross McNaughton, an Australian member of the Marilyn Monroe fandom community, members of Immortal Marilyn coordinated a fundraising effort in order to have a plaque with his name on it placed at Westwood Cemetery, near Marilyn's crypt. (© Immortal Marilyn)

ing from all over the world. We exchange birthday and Christmas cards, make plans to meet with one another, trade pieces from our collections. There is a sense of camaraderie that cannot be faked or replicated. The community as a whole is quite diverse. There are groups that share photos, that strictly discuss her film career, that focus on her relationships. There are countless subcategories of study and discussion of her. The more serious fans tend to congregate among themselves on smaller pages in order to have the kind of in-depth discussions and personal relationships with other fans that simply cannot be found on the larger sites.

The positive impact of MM fandom: [Fandom] means I'm not alone. It means I have an identity and can contribute to something I'm passionate about. It's an outlet to talk about a subject that I adore but that most people couldn't care less about. It means friendships with some of the most genuine and kind people I've ever had the pleasure to know, friendships that have deepened far beyond our love of Marilyn into true kinships.

[Fandom] has impacted my life immeasurably. I went from being a fan, reading books and watching films all by myself to having an enormous community of people with the exact same fascination with Marilyn that I do. It's remarkable to spend decades thinking you're the only one to then find that there are hundreds – if not thousands – of people who thought they were the only ones too. When you discover one another, it feels like you've found long-lost friends. It has also impacted my life in that I've built a name for myself within the community as someone knowledgeable, someone who does good research, and it made me rediscover my love for writing that I had abandoned since high school. I find fulfillment in it. My days are spent cooking, cleaning and caring for two small children (one with special needs)... the fan community helps give me a sense of identity and worth outside of simply being a housewife.

New Developments in MM Fandom: Lately there has been an absolutely huge increase in the number of people joining the fan groups, sometimes as many as 500 new members in a week. I'm not sure where this resurgence of interest in Marilyn has come from lately, but it's nice to see that she keeps appealing to new generations. Another new and more troubling development is that lately there seems to be an epidemic of attributing fake quotes to Marilyn and altering photos of her (i.e. putting her

Fig. 3: Marijane Gray at the gates of Marilyn Monroe's home (© Marijane Gray)

Fig. 4: A luncheon at Twentieth Century Fox studios for the members of the Immortal Marilyn Fan Club during the 50th Anniversary Memorial, 2012 (© Marijane Gray).

head onto someone else's body). Some might not think either of these are a big deal, but Marilyn herself spoke out about not wanting anything she didn't say being attributed to her, so the fake quotes are not only disrespectful to her wishes, but also, they present a completely false image of her to newer fans. The real person that she was gets lost amidst a variety of trite sayings with her name attached to them. It's the same with the altered pictures: newer fans no longer know what is false and what is genuine, and the real Marilyn who was admirable in her own right is lost to these false representations of her. Another problem with this is that fake quotes and altered photos are being marketed and sold, and fans are none too happy when they find out they've spent their money on something that wasn't genuine Marilyn.

Marilyn's Legacy for her Fans: Marilyn was always very kind and gracious to her fans, giving them the credit for making her a star. 'If I'm a star, then the people made me a star' – the people continue to keep her a star, keep her light shining. We are all drawn to different aspects of her and relate to different facets of her personality. Some love her glamour, some love her tenacity and ambition against seemingly insurmountable odds, and some want to protect her. She once compared herself to a mirror, saying that people saw reflections of themselves in her. It was very astute when she said it, and it holds true today. Ultimately, Marilyn's legacy is iconic and legendary. Those that look beyond the skirt flying up and a breathy rendition of 'Happy Birthday' find a woman who was smart, sensitive, kind and way ahead of her time. That is her legacy… each time a new fan discovers who she really was beyond the Cinemascope and the scandal, and sees her for the remarkable woman she really was, each time she inspires a young girl to think that if the most beautiful woman of all time could be self conscious and insecure then it's okay if they are too, each

Fan Appreciation no.6
Marijane Gray

time someone realizes this supposed 'dumb blonde' was far from dumb, Marilyn has cemented her legacy as an unrivalled icon that much more. As each new generation of fans discovers who she truly was, she ensures her own immortality. ●

(Answers have been condensed and edited)

Biographical note
Marijane Gray is a stay-at-home mother who writes research/investigative articles about Marilyn Monroe for the highly respected *Immortal-Marilyn.com* as well as for Buzzfeed.com and *Yahoo! News*. She frequently answers fan questions about her as well as assists collectors with authenticating and appraising Marilyn memorabilia and collectibles. Marijane attended numerous Marilyn events in Los Angeles in 2012 for the 50th Anniversary Memorial.

~~~~~~~~~~

GO FURTHER

Books
Marilyn & I
Yury Toroptsov, preface by Catherine Deneuve
(Paris: Verlhac, 2011)

Online
Articles
'Fans Angry Over Facebook Page Removal, ABG'
Elisa Jordan interview with Marijane Gray
Examiner.com. 22 March 2012, http://www.examiner.com/article/fans-angry-over-facebook-page-removal-abg.

'Facebook and the Ownership of Marilyn Monroe'
Marijane Gray
Yahoo! Voices. 9 March 2012,
http://voices.yahoo.com/facebook-ownership-marilyn-monroe-11069466.html?cat=15.
'For the Love of Ross.' Tribute to Ross McNaughton, *Immortal Marilyn* (n.d.), http://www.immortalmarilyn.com/ForTheLoveofRoss.html.

'Misquoting Marilyn'
Marijane Gray
Immortal Marilyn (n.d.), http://www.immortalmarilyn.com/
MisquotingMMGray.html.
'The Myths of August Fifth'
Marijane Gray
Immortal Marilyn (n.d.), http://www.immortalmarilyn.com/
TwilightTheMythsOfAugustFifth.html.

'The Underestimation of Marilyn Monroe'
Marijane Gray
Immortal Marilyn (n.d.), http://www.immortalmarilyn.com/
MarijaneGrayMM2.html.

Films
The Seven Year Itch, Billy Wilder, dir. (United States: Twentieth Century
Fox, 1955).

Editor and Contributor Details

EDITOR

Marcelline Block (BA, Harvard; MA, Princeton; Ph.D. cand., Princeton) is the editor of *World Film Locations: Paris* (Intellect, 2011), *World Film Locations: Las Vegas* (Intellect, 2012), *World Film Locations: Prague* (Intellect, 2013), *World Film Locations: Marseilles* (Intellect, 2013) and its French translation/Expanded version, *Filmer Marseille* (Presses universitaires de Provence, 2013), *World Film Locations: Boston* (Intellect, 2014) and *Situating the Feminist Gaze and Spectatorship in Postwar Cinema* (Cambridge Scholars Publishing, 2008; 2nd edn 2010), which was translated into Italian as *Sguardo e pubblico femminista nel cinema del dopoguerra* (Aracne editrice, 2012). She is also the co-editor of *The Directory of World Cinema: Belgium* (Intellect, 2014) and *Unequal Before Death* (Cambridge Scholars, 2012), both of which were awarded publication grants from Columbia University. Her articles and book chapters about film, literature and visual art have appeared in English, Chinese, French, Italian and Russian. She has held teaching positions at Princeton University and lectured about Paris in Cinema at 92Y TriBeCa, New York City.

CONTRIBUTORS

Raquel Crisóstomo teaches in the Communication Sciences Faculty at the Internacional University of Catalonia, in the studies of advertising, audiovisual communication and journalism. She has been professor of a serial narrative course for three years at the Faculty of Humanities at the University Pompeu Fabra. Her Ph.D. in Humanities at the Pompeu Fabra University (2011), was titled *Art Spiegelman's Maus: A Dissociation of Roles through the Semiotic Genealogy of Cats and Mice in Literature, The Graphic Novel and Visual Culture*. Crisóstomo's research area covers comics and the serial narrative in general, most especially television fiction from the perspective of cultural studies. She has published several academic articles on television serials. With Enric Ros, she is currently editing a book about *Mad Men*.

Louise Elali is a Brazilian-born journalist (Universidade Potiguar, Brazil) and psychologist (Universidade Federal do Rio Grande do Norte, Brazil), with a Master's degree in Global Visual Communication at Jacobs University Bremen (Germany). Her interests are highly interdisciplinary, in particular considering the intersection between Communication Studies and Psychology, especially in the realms of entertainment and mass media (in its many forms), and their lasting effects in the viewers.

Considered an authority on Marilyn Monroe, **Scott Fortner** assists major auction companies in authenticating and verifying memorabilia, Marilyn Monroe-owned items and Marilyn Monroe autographs. Fortner is often called upon by worldwide news agencies, including the AP, BBC and Reuters, to comment on Monroe topics. In 2010, Fortner was showcased in a feature photography project, 'Marilyn & I', shot by French photographer Yury Toroptsov, and the photos were exhibited in Paris in 2011. He was a guest of the Academy of Motion Picture Arts and Sciences, where he presented to a packed audience for an exclusive viewing of behind-the-scenes footage of Marilyn from *Bus Stop* (Joshua Logan, 1956), as part of 'Hollywood Home Movies III: Treasures from the Academy Film Archive Collection'. Also in 2011, Fortner was showcased in the independent documentary, *With Her*, which was produced and directed by French film-maker Laurent Morlet. In 2012, he was the featured speaker at 'Tonner Air', the annual spring convention held by the Tonner Doll Company, where their first ever Marilyn Monroe dolls were unveiled.

Tara Hanks was born and raised in London. Since then she has lived in Lancaster, Derby and now Brighton. *Wicked Baby*, Tara's novella based on the events of the Profumo Affair, was published in 2005. An extract has been showcased on the official website of Whitbread-nominated author Laura Hird. *The MMM Girl*, Tara's novel about the life of Marilyn Monroe, is winner of the UKA Press Opening Pages Competition, and was pub-

Editor and Contributor Details

lished in 2007 by UKA Press. An excerpt is featured in *Voices from the Web Anthology 2006* (UKA Press). Tara also writes about aspects of popular culture and maintains the *Everlasting Star Updates* blog.

Zachary Ingle is a Ph.D. candidate in Film and Media Studies at the University of Kansas where he is completing a dissertation exploring Robert Rodriguez. He has written for several volumes in Intellect's World Film Locations series, including *Boston* (2014), *Las Vegas* (2012), *Marseilles* (2013), *Paris* (2011), *Prague* (2013) and *Shanghai* (2014). Other work appearing in Intellect Books include Directory of World Cinema books devoted to *Sweden, Belgium, Australia and New Zealand* (Vol. 2), *Japan* (Vol. 3) and *American Independent* (Vol. 3), as well as *Fan Phenomena: Star Wars* (Intellect, 2013). Ingle has also edited four books: *Robert Rodriguez: Interviews* (University Press of Mississippi, 2012), *Fan Phenomena: The Big Lebowski* (Intellect, 2014), *Gender and Genre in Sports Documentaries* (Scarecrow Press, 2013) and *Identity and Myth in Sports Documentaries* (Scarecrow Press, 2013). His work has appeared in journals such as *Literature/Film Quarterly, Journal of Sport History, Film & History, Journal of American Culture, Mass Communication and Society, Film-Philosophy* and *Journal of Religion and Film.*

Ross Sloan is a lecturer in the Department of English at Southern Methodist University in Dallas, Texas, where he lives with his wife and seven children. Creative writing aside, his scholarship has mostly focused on comic studies, media studies and popular culture studies. In 2012 he taught a course titled, 'Fame Monsters: Thinking and Writing about Celebrity Culture in the Age of Gaga'. The readings and concepts explored in that course contributed to his essay on Marilyn Monroe as a woman transcending both reality and mortality. The students from that spring semester remain the finest he has ever met and taught; they are the gold standard. Though it is uncommon to dedicate an essay in an anthology to anyone, this essay is dedicated to each of the sixty of them for being so lovable and inspirational. Also to Emily, my knockout of a wife! Not every brunette would tolerate her husband spending long hours at the library thinking deeply about a voluptuous blonde.

Catalina Vázquez is a multimedia journalist (University of Oregon) who focuses on the representation of marginalized people in big media. Born and raised in sunny California, she has covered everything from undocumented migration to the historical role of converse chucks in street culture. Her intense curiosity is what contributed to her first degree in Ethnic Studies and Intermedia Arts (Mills College) and second Master's in Global Visual Communication (Jacobs University Bremen). She gears her focus to the intersection of media and politics, paying great attention to the people and movements who redefine their social limitations.

Ange Webb is a freelance writer who has recently completed a British Contemporary Fiction course to add to her other qualifications, which include a postgraduate certificate in English Literature Studies from Oxford Brookes. She also studied Modern English Poetry there. Published work and conference presentations include arts reviews and film articles. Ange worked for many years at the Bodleian Library. Her critical interests include Marilyn Monroe; cinema history, particularly the Golden Age of Hollywood; vintage clothes; 1950s–1960s alternative culture; fan phenomena; and glossy magazines.

'MARILYN MONROE
IS SO MUCH MORE
THAN AN ACTRESS.
SHE IS A SYMBOL,
A LEGEND,
AN ICON OF AMERICA
AND FOR AMERICA.
THIS IS MARILYN.'

THISISMARILYN.COM,
A SOCIAL NETWORK FOR MARILYN MONROE FANS